Macarons

Tan Phay Shing

mc Marshall Cavendish
Cuisine

The publisher would like to thank Phoon Huat & Co Pte Ltd
and Chew's Group Limited for their support of this publication.

Editor: Lydia Leong
Designer: Adithi Khandadai
All photos by Hongde Photography except step-by-step photos by Tan Phay Shing

Published by Marshall Cavendish Cuisine
An imprint of Marshall Cavendish International

Other Marshall Cavendish Offices:
Marshall Cavendish Corporation. 99 White Plains Road, Tarrytown NY 10591-9001, USA •
Marshall Cavendish International (Thailand) Co Ltd. 253 Asoke, 12th Flr, Sukhumvit 21 Road,
Klongtoey Nua, Wattana, Bangkok 10110, Thailand • Marshall Cavendish (Malaysia) Sdn Bhd,
Times Subang, Lot 46, Subang Hi-Tech Industrial Park, Batu Tiga, 40000 Shah Alam,
Selangor Darul Ehsan, Malaysia

Marshall Cavendish is a trademark of Times Publishing Limited

National Library Board, Singapore Cataloguing in Publication Data

Names: Tan, Phay Shing, author. | Leong, Lydia, editor.
Title: Creative baking : macarons / Tan Phay Shing ; editor, Lydia Leong.
Description: Singapore : Marshall Cavendish Cuisine, [2016]
Identifiers: OCN 933496782 | ISBN 978-981-47-2141-7 (paperback)
Subjects: LCSH: Macarons. | GSAFD: Cookbooks.
Classification: LCC TX772 | DDC 641.8654--dc23

Printed by Times Offset (M) Sdn Bhd

Dedication

To my husband Jianlong,
our children Mun Yew and Mun Zhong,
and my mum and dad

Contents

My Favourite Things

Around Town

Animal Friends

Back to Nature

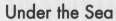
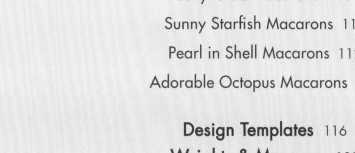

Under the Sea

Acknowledgements

First and foremost, I would like to thank God for providing me with the inspiration and energy to bake while taking care of the kids, cooking for the family and doing the housework.

I am immensely thankful for the support my husband gives me, whether it is by being my guinea pig for taste testing and giving his brutally honest feedback, providing the kitchen equipment I need, or going out of his way to help me source for natural food colouring products.

I am thankful that my children are excellent at telling me what looks cute or not and encouraging me when I encounter failed or difficult bakes.

I am also grateful to my parents for their support and for providing practical help, such as washing up after I bake.

I would also like to thank:

Vanessa, a very talented home cook and baker for inspiring me to begin my creative macaron journey and providing guidance along the way, especially when I was new to baking macarons.

Susanne, my friend and baking partner for her friendship and encouragement as we travel together in this creative baking journey.

Lydia, my editor for giving me this opportunity to do this book, for her endless patience and support, and for being so accommodating. I could not have asked for a better editor!

Adithi the designer and Hongde the photographer for their professionalism and creativity in making the photography sessions fun and enjoyable, and making the macarons look so beautiful!

Phoon Huat & Co Pte Ltd and Chew's Group Limited — my favourite ingredient suppliers — for their kind support of this book.

Introduction

Macarons! You either love them or hate them. This delicate French confectionery has a reputation of being difficult to master, despite being made up of only almond powder, sugar and egg whites. Yet, they have an irresistible draw for me, a person who does not have a sweet tooth and who used to shy away from making meringues, the base of macarons, for fear of failure!

I was first inspired to try making macarons when I saw the beautiful creations of some home bakers. Desiring to do the same, I put aside my fears and whipped up an initial batch of macarons. But what came out of the oven looked more like tuiles! The mixture had spread to almost twice the size of the dollop that I had piped and there were many tiny holes all over the surface. Undeterred, and with the advice of an experienced fellow baker, Vanessa, I tried again and again, until I found my groove.

Besides making pretty macarons, I also enjoy making special fillings to go with the shells. I like pairing the shells with fillings that are savoury or sour to create delicacies that are light, full of flavour and not too sweet, and which will almost melt in your mouth.

I hope this book will inspire you to try your hand at making macarons, and not just round ones, but beautiful works of art that taste as good as they look! Don't be discouraged if your early attempts don't turn out well. With practise, you will get better! Just have fun!

Happy baking!

Phay Shing

Basic Tools & Equipment

Electric Mixer

An electric mixer is useful for whipping up the meringue which forms the base of macarons. You can use either a handheld or stand mixer, but for the former, you will need a heavy mixing bowl as these recipes are prepared with Italian meringue which will require you to add the boiling syrup while whisking the egg whites. A lightweight bowl may spin around as you beat the egg whites.

Mixing Bowls

Having several mixing bowls of different sizes will be handy when making macarons. You will need a large mixing bowl for whisking the meringue and a medium one for mixing the mass (mixture of almond powder, icing sugar and egg white). Smaller bowls will be useful for mixing batter of different colours.

A stainless steel mixing bowl is best for whisking the meringue. Wipe the bowl with a paper towel and some lemon juice or vinegar to remove any residual grease as the presence of grease may affect the foaming properties of the egg whites.

Sieve

It is necessary to sift almond flour, icing sugar and other powdered ingredients such as cocoa powder and food colouring to break up any lumps and aerate the mixture. Large pieces of almond that are unable to pass through the fine mesh of the sieve should be discarded to ensure that the macaron shells have a smooth surface.

Kitchen Scale

Ingredients have to be weighed with precision for the macarons to turn out well consistently. Measuring the ingredients by volume using cups and spoons introduces more variation between batches of macarons. Choose a digital weighing scale that is able to measure at least 1 g as the smallest unit of measurement.

5 Candy Thermometer

I use the Italian meringue method of making macarons using hot sugar syrup and it is necessary to measure the temperature of the syrup before adding it to the egg whites. Hence, a candy thermometer or sugar thermometer is essential. The syrup needs to reach 115°C, also known as the soft ball stage, before it can be incorporated into the egg whites.

6 Oven Thermometer

It is helpful to have an oven thermometer in the oven throughout the baking time so you can monitor the temperature and ensure the macarons bake evenly. Macarons made using the Italian meringue method are typically baked at temperatures ranging from 130°C–140°C.

Light coloured shells are typically baked at a slightly lower temperature for a longer time to prevent the shells from browning while making sure that they are thoroughly cooked inside. An oven thermometer will allow you to have better control of the actual temperature of the oven for different coloured shells. Do bear in mind that individual ovens work differently, so learn to understand your oven and adjust the baking times and temperatures as necessary.

7 Baking Paper

I line the baking trays with baking paper when making macarons, so it is not necessary to use a silicone baking mat if you do not already own one. Choose heavy-duty baking paper that is non-stick and heat-resistant for the best results.

8 Baking Trays

Any type of metal baking tray that fits into your oven is suitable, although different metals conduct heat differently, so you may want to monitor your first batch of macarons more carefully.

Have several baking trays on hand as the recipes make 80–100 shells, depending on size, and the piped batter needs to be left on the trays to dry before baking.

The design templates provided in this book are meant to be enlarged by 200% on the photocopier, and printed on A4 size paper. Place the template on the baking tray under the sheet of baking paper. Baking trays that can fit an A4 sheet comfortably will do. For these recipes, I used trays measuring 35-cm x 25-cm.

Spatula

Choose a spatula with a firm wooden handle or a very stiff plastic handle to enable you to better handle the mass (mixture of almond powder, icing sugar and egg white) as it has a very thick consistency.

Piping Tips and Piping Bags

Round piping tips 4–7 mm in diameter are typically used for piping the base shells. Smaller piping tips 1–3 mm in diameter are used for piping features on the base shells. It is useful to have multiple piping tips of the same size on hand if working with various colours of batter.

I usually use small disposable plastic piping bags when piping fancy shapes for better control. Disposable bags also do away with the need for washing multiple bags if working with various colours of batter.

Toothpicks

In making creative macarons, toothpicks are used for nudging piped macaron batter into tight corners to create a more defined shape, or for pulling the batter to create fine features that stick out from the main shell body. Toothpicks are also used for nudging royal icing into tight corners or painting fine royal icing features onto baked shells.

Edible Ink Markers

Besides piping features on the baked shells using royal icing, edible ink markers can also be used for drawing fine features. As the ink may smudge when in contact with moisture, do not use markers to draw on royal icing for macarons that require refrigeration. The ink may also transfer and it is thus advisable not to stack the macarons if using ink markers.

Basic Ingredients

Almond Powder (Superfine)

This finely ground powder is a key ingredient in making macarons. Almond powder made from blanched almonds will ensure a more even colour for your macarons as the brown almond skin has been removed. Choose almond powder that has been very finely ground (superfine) so it is easier to sift. You may choose to grind your own almonds, but buying them already ground saves time. Almond powder can also be substituted with other ground nuts such as hazelnuts, cashews and pecans.

Icing Sugar

Also known as confectioner's sugar, this fine, powdered sugar is another main ingredient in making macarons. Some manufacturers mix cornstarch into the icing sugar to prevent clumping, and I have used both pure icing sugar or icing sugar with cornstarch to make macarons and found no significant difference in the quality of the macarons.

Sugar

Any type of granulated white sugar is suitable for making macarons using the Italian meringue method as the sugar will be dissolved to make the hot syrup.

Egg Whites

Fresh or aged egg whites are both suitable when using the Italian meringue method for making macarons. However, I find that separating the eggs in advance saves me time on the day I plan to bake. If you prefer to age your egg whites, place them in a bowl, cover with a paper towel and refrigerate for 1–2 days. Always let the egg whites come to room temperature before using.

Food Colouring

Use gel or powdered food colouring but not liquid food colouring in macaron batter to avoid introducing liquid into the batter. Liquid will hinder proper drying of the shells. I prefer to use natural food colouring although the colours tend to be subdued and may need to be enhanced using artificial colouring. In these recipes, I use both natural food colouring and gel food colouring.

Basic Macaron Recipe

The yield of this recipe will vary with the size and shape of the macarons. As a rough guide, these quantities will produce batter sufficient for 80–100 shells or 40–50 macarons.

 Scan the QR code to view a video tutorial on preparing macarons.

Mass
200 g almond powder

200 g icing sugar

80 g egg whites, at room temperature

Desired gel food colouring

Italian Meringue
80 g egg whites, at room temperature

200 g sugar

75 g water

1. Place paper template on baking tray and line with baking paper. When Italian meringue is ready, dab some on four corners of baking tray to keep baking paper from moving around.

2. Prepare mass. Sift together almond powder and icing sugar. Add egg whites and mix well. Add a little food colouring and mix well. Bear in mind that the shade will lighten when meringue is folded in.

3. Prepare Italian meringue. In a clean, grease-free mixing bowl, beat egg whites at medium-low speed until foamy and opaque, and any peaks that form are soft and melt back into themselves after a second. This is known as the soft peak stage. Do not beat past this stage or the meringue will be too stiff to incorporate into the mass. Reduce mixer speed if necessary to keep egg whites moving.

4. While egg whites are beating, heat sugar and water in a small saucepan until mixture reaches 115°C on a candy thermometer. Stop stirring once sugar has dissolved to avoid crystals forming. Remove from heat immediately when temperature is reached.

5. Turn mixer speed to medium-high. Slowly and carefully pour hot syrup into egg whites, taking care to avoid whisk. When syrup has been incorporated, increase to high speed and beat for about 10 minutes or until meringue cools to 50°C or less. You should get stiff, glossy peaks when whisk is slowly lifted. Reserve a tablespoonful of meringue for sticking baking paper on baking tray.

6. Prepare macaron batter. Fold Italian meringue into mass. You do not have to be too gentle when folding as the meringue needs to be deflated slightly to obtain the right consistency.

7. Using a spatula and starting from the right (7a), bring batter from bottom of bowl up to the other side (7b). Flip batter over (7c), then press spatula downwards and towards side of bowl nearest you (7d). Repeat steps, turning mixing bowl slowly as you fold.

8. When batter looks evenly mixed and there are no traces of meringue, test to see if consistency is right. Scoop a generous dollop of batter and watch how it falls back into the mixing bowl. An under-mixed batter will fall in a discontinuous manner. Continue folding several more times and test again.

9. When the batter falls off the spatula in a slow, magma-like way, forming a ribbon but breaking off at a few points, it is ready for piping fancy shaped macarons. If piping round macarons, continue folding until batter is just able to fall off the spatula in an almost continuous ribbon, breaking off at a couple of points. Be careful not to overfold, or the batter will be too runny and the macarons won't turn out well.

10. Transfer batter to a piping bag fitted with a 4–7 mm round tip to pipe shells. Use smaller piping tips (1–3 mm) for piping fine details. Place piping bag over a tall mug. Pour or scoop batter in. Although macaron batter is stable, it is best to transfer it into the piping bag as soon as it is ready or keep it covered with plastic wrap touching the surface of the batter to prevent a crust forming.

11. Pipe shells on baking paper using paper template as a guide. Hold piping bag perpendicular to tray, with tip 6–7 mm away from baking paper. Press piping bag lightly to start piping (11a). When done, release pressure on piping bag and give a little twirl before lifting tip off (11b).

12. Hold baking paper down and tap tray hard on table top several times to release trapped air bubbles. Peaks will flatten with tapping.

13. Leave shells to dry for 1–2 hours, or until shells are dry to the touch and do not stick to your finger when you run it across the surface. In hot and humid climates, you may need to let the shells dry in an air-conditioned room or well-ventilated place with a fan. Baking when the piped batter is still sticky will result in cracked shells (13a). Leaving the piped batter out to dry for too long will result in poor feet formation (13b).

14. Preheat oven and bake shells, rotating tray halfway through baking. Use an oven thermometer to monitor temperature of oven.

    For light coloured shells, including white and any pastel colours, bake at 130°C for 17–22 minutes with baking tray on lowest rack.

    For bright and strong coloured shells, bake at 135°C for 17–20 minutes with baking tray on lowest or second lowest rack.

    For dark coloured shells, including black and dark brown, bake at 140°C for 16–20 minutes with baking tray on second lowest rack.

15. Remove from oven and let shells cool on tray before removing by gently peeling baking paper away from shells.

16. If feet appear a little wet, return tray to oven and bake at 120°C for another 5 minutes before checking again. Do not attempt to remove shells from baking sheet if they are stuck as this means they are under baked (16a). If shells appear to be browning, check that oven temperature has not exceeded 120°C. Bake for a few minutes and check again.

17. Store cooled shells in an airtight container if not using immediately.

18. After decorating and/or filling, let shells sit in an airtight container in the refrigerator, or in a cool, dry place for non-refrigerated fillings, for at least 24 hours before serving.

19. The shells can be prepared in advance and kept frozen for up to 3 months. To freeze shells, place between layers of baking paper in an airtight container. Thaw at room temperature without opening container. Decorate and/or fill as desired.

20. Prepare desired filling and spoon into small piping bag. Cut a small hole at the tip. Pipe filling onto half the shells and sandwich with other half.

21. If using 2 types of filling, pipe a ring of filling on shell (21a), then pipe other type of filling in centre (21b).

13a

13b

16a

20

21a

21b

Piping Macarons

Piping macarons will be easy once you master a few basic piping techniques. Hold the piping bag perpendicular to the tray, with the tip 6–7 mm away. Apply gently pressure on the piping bag to start piping.

Scan the QR code to view video tutorials on piping basic macarons shapes such as ovals, rectangles and triangles.

Oval

This is perhaps the most common shape in making creative macarons. Start by piping an oval within the boundary of the template. Fill the centre of the oval with batter and end by lifting the tip from the centre of the piped batter. It is not necessary to pipe to the edges of the template as the batter will spread slightly. Tap the tray firmly on the table top several times to flatten any peaks.

Narrow Rectangle

Using a 5–7 mm piping tip, pipe a straight line within the boundary of the template. The size of the tip will depend on the width of the line you wish to pipe. End by lifting the tip from the centre of the piped batter. Use a toothpick to pull the batter into the corners of the rectangle. For rounded corners, skip this step. Tap the tray firmly on the table top several times to smoothen any unevenness.

Broad Rectangle

Pipe a rectangle within the boundary of the template. Fill the centre of the rectangle with batter and end by lifting the tip from the centre of the piped batter. It is not necessary to pipe to the edges of the template as the batter will spread slightly. Use a toothpick to pull the batter into the corners of the rectangle. For rounded corners, skip this step. Tap the tray firmly on the table top several times to smoothen any unevenness.

Triangle

  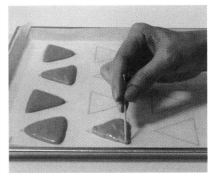

Pipe a triangle within the boundary of the template. Fill the centre of the triangle with batter and end by lifting the tip from the centre of the piped batter. It is not necessary to pipe to the edges of the template as the batter will spread slightly. Use a toothpick to pull the batter into the corners of the triangle. For rounded corners, skip this step. Tap the tray firmly on the table top several times to smoothen any unevenness.

Scan the QR code to view video tutorials on piping complex shapes and 3D features, as well as creating fine features.

Complex Shapes (Trace-and-fill Technique)

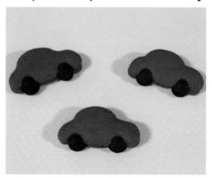  

Complex shapes can be piped using the trace-and-fill technique. This technique is also used for piping non-circular shapes. Start by piping the outline of the shape, then fill in any spaces and the centre with batter. End by lifting the tip from the centre of the piped batter. Use a toothpick to pull the batter into the corners of the shape. Tap the tray firmly on the table top several times to smoothen any unevenness.

Complex Shapes (Combining Simple Shapes)

Complex shapes can also be formed by breaking down the shape into smaller, simple shapes. Using the shape of a cloud as an example, start by piping a circle within the template, followed by another circle next to it. Continue piping circles to complete the shape, then fill in any spaces and the centre with batter. End by lifting the tip from the centre of the piped batter. Tap the tray firmly on the table top several times to smoothen any unevenness.

3D Features

3D features such as snouts and limbs can be created after the base has been left to dry for about 15 minutes or until a sticky membrane forms on the surface. At this point, the base should feel a little sticky, but the batter should not stick to your finger when you touch the base gently. Use a small round tip to pipe the 3D features.

Fine Features

Fine features such as pointy ears or hair can be created after the base has been smoothened by tapping the tray on the table top. Use a toothpick to gently pull the batter to create the desired effect.

Natural Food Colouring Guide

Macaron batters can be coloured using gel or natural food colouring, with the colouring added to the mass (rather than the meringue) so there is the flexibility of making more than one coloured batter in a batch without having to make multiple portions of meringue. It is also easier to adjust the colour of the mass to obtain the desired shade, as once the meringue is added, making adjustments may lead to over-folding.

Some natural food colouring comes in powdered form. You can also extract colouring from natural ingredients. This guide provides suggestions on natural sources of colouring and explains how to use them.

Red

Beetroot and Red Yeast Powders

Dissolve beetroot powder in egg whites for mass. Sift red yeast powder with almond powder and icing sugar. Mix with coloured egg whites. Does not add flavour to shells.

Pink

Natural Pink Powder (Beetroot-based)

Sift with almond powder and icing sugar, then mix with egg whites. Does not add flavour to shells.

Orange

Carrot Powder

Sift with almond powder and icing sugar then mix with egg whites. Does not add flavour to shells.

Yellow

Natural Sourced Yellow Powder (Tumeric-based)

Sift with almond powder and icing sugar, then mix with egg whites. Does not add flavour to shells.

Purple

Purple Sweet Potato Powder

Sift with almond powder and icing sugar,
then mix with egg whites.
Does not add flavour to shells.

Black

Charcoal Powder

Sift with almond powder and icing sugar,
then mix with egg whites.
Does not add flavour to shells.

Brown

Cocoa Powder or Earl Grey Tea Powder

Sift with almond powder and icing sugar,
then mix with egg whites.
Both sources add flavour to shells.

Green

Matcha Powder or Natural Green Powder (Chlorophyll-based)

Sift with almond powder and icing sugar, then mix
with egg whites. You get matcha flavoured shells
if matcha powder is used. The natural sourced
green powder does not add flavour to shells.

Blue

Dried Blue Pea Flowers

Steep about 1 Tbsp dried blue pea flowers
per 80 g egg whites for 1 hour. Strain and
top up with more egg whites to make up weight
specified in recipe. Sift together almond powder and
icing sugar, then mix with coloured egg whites.
Does not add flavour to the shells.

Basic Royal Icing

After the macarons have been baked, it's time to start decorating! Royal icing can be prepared in a variety of colours to create fine details on macarons.

250 g icing sugar

18 g meringue powder

43 g cool boiled water

A few drops of vanilla extract or other flavouring (optional)

Gel food colouring

> *Note* Royal icing is typically off-white in colour. Use white gel food colouring to make it pure white if desired.
>
> For black royal icing, use charcoal powder.
>
> For brown royal icing, use cocoa powder with a bit of brown gel food colouring.

1. Sift together icing sugar and meringue powder into a mixing bowl. Gradually add water and flavouring, if using, and beat with a hand whisk for 5–6 minutes, or with a handheld electric mixer for 3 minutes on low speed.

2. Test consistency by lifting whisk and allowing icing to fall back into bowl. Any peaks in the icing should disappear in about 10 seconds. Adjust consistency if necessary by adding more water or icing sugar.

3. Colour icing as desired.

4. Transfer icing into a piping bag fitted with a fine piping tip. Use as desired.

5. Use a toothpick to ease icing into small corners or for drawing very fine details.

6. Royal icing will keep refrigerated for up to 1 month. Store in an airtight container with plastic wrap touching the surface of icing. Stir well before use.

Macaron Fillings

Macarons can be filled with an endless variety of fillings, and here are some of my favourites. They are full of flavour and not too sweet. I have categorised them as Refrigerated and Non-refrigerated Fillings, the latter being fillings that do not require refrigeration and which will stand up well in warmer climates.

After the macarons are filled, set them aside at least 24 hours before consuming. This will allow the macarons to mature and the flavours of the filling to infuse the shell.

Refrigerated Fillings

Chocolate Ganache

150 g milk or dark chocolate,
very finely chopped

10 g butter, cut into small pieces

75 g whipping cream

1. Place chocolate and butter in a heatproof bowl. Heat cream in a saucepan over low heat until it starts to bubble.

2. Pour hot cream over chocolate and butter (2a). Use a spatula to stir mixture in a single direction until smooth (2b). If lumps of chocolate remain, place bowl over a simmering pot of water and continue stirring until chocolate is completely melted. Make sure water does not touch base of bowl.

3. Let ganache rest at room temperature for 1 hour or until firm before using.

Lemon Curd

45 g unsalted butter
at room temperature

112 g castor sugar

1 large egg (65 g)

1 large egg yolk

80 g freshly squeezed lemon juice

½ tsp finely grated lemon zest

1. Using an electric mixer, beat butter and sugar at medium speed for about 2 minutes until creamy. Gradually add egg and egg yolk and beat for 1 minute. Mix in lemon juice. Mixture will appear to curdle, but this is fine.

2. Cook mixture over low heat, stirring constantly until smooth. Increase heat to medium and keep stirring until mixture thickens and coats the back of a wooden spoon. Do not let mixture boil. Remove from heat and stir in lemon zest.

3. Transfer to a bowl and press plastic wrap on surface of curd to keep skin from forming. Chill before use. Lemon curd will keep for up to a week refrigerated and up to 2 months in the freezer.

Salted Caramel with Flavour Variations

60 g heavy cream

100 g sugar

2 Tbsp water

15 g unsalted butter

1 tsp sea salt

Optional flavours

1 Earl Grey teabag
  (for Earl Grey tea flavour)

$1/2$ tsp ground cinnamon
  (for cinnamon flavour)

$1/8$ tsp ground ginger
  (for ginger flavour)

1. If making Earl Grey tea-flavoured salted caramel, heat heavy cream in a saucepan over low heat until it starts to bubble. Remove from heat. Add teabag and leave to infuse until cream is a warm tan colour. Squeeze cream from teabag and discard teabag. Skip this step if making spiced salted caramel.

2. Place sugar and water in a deep, light coloured saucepan so colour of syrup will be visible. Cook over medium heat without stirring until golden brown in colour. Watch solution carefully to avoid burning. You may gently swirl the solution in the saucepan for it to cook more evenly.

3. Turn off heat and carefully add cream while stirring with a long wooden spoon. The mixture will bubble up (3a). Keep stirring until mixture settles (3b).

4. Add butter and salt. If making spiced salted caramel, add either spice. Mix well.

5. Set aside to cool before using. Store in an airtight container. Salted caramel will keep for up to a week refrigerated or up to 3 months in the freezer.

Basic Vanilla Swiss Meringue Buttercream (SMBC)

Swiss meringue buttercream is often used as a base for different flavours of macaron filling because it is light and versatile. Here is a basic recipe for a low sugar version which goes perfectly with the sweet shells. This recipe makes about 250 g.

Jazz it up with your favourite ingredients. I have provided some suggestions to vary the basic buttercream in the following pages. The quantities can be adjusted according to taste.

75 g egg whites (from 2 large eggs)

A pinch of salt

50 g castor sugar

135 g unsalted butter, at room temperature, cut into cubes

1 tsp vanilla extract

Note To speed up the cooling of the meringue at step 4, I usually place a cool damp towel under the bowl and have a standing fan blowing on it.

1. Prepare a deep saucepan and a heatproof bowl that will sit snugly into the mouth of the saucepan.

2. Fill pan with water to a depth of 2.5 cm and place over low heat. Place egg whites, salt and sugar in heatproof bowl and place into pan.

3. Using a hand whisk or handheld electric mixer, whisk egg whites at medium-low speed for 5–6 minutes until sugar has melted and mixture is foamy. The temperature should read 71.1°C on a candy thermometer.

4. Remove bowl from heat and continue beating at high speed for about 10 minutes until mixture is stiff and glossy, and has cooled to 30°C. Scrape down sides of bowl from time to time to ensure mixture is even.

5. Add a cube of butter and beat at medium speed until butter is incorporated. Do not worry if mixture appears to curdle. Continue adding butter a cube at a time. When all the butter has been added, increase speed and beat for 1–2 minutes until mixture is light and fluffy. Add vanilla extract and beat well until incorporated. Use as desired.

6. Swiss meringue buttercream can be prepared up to a month in advance. Place in a resealable plastic bag and store in the freezer. Bring to room temperature and whisk until light and fluffy before using.

Strawberry SMBC

250 g Swiss meringue buttercream
40–50 g strawberry purée
$\frac{1}{2}$ tsp strawberry paste

Place buttercream in a bowl and gradually mix in strawberry purée. Do not add more purée than suggested amount as cream will become too soft.

Note: Strawberry purée can be prepared by pressing fresh or thawed frozen strawberries through a wire mesh sieve. Other types of berries such as raspberries and blackberries can also be used.

Lemon SMBC

250 g Swiss meringue buttercream
85 g lemon curd (page 31)

Place buttercream in a bowl and gradually mix in lemon curd.

Note: This cream offers a strong lemon flavour without adding moisture to the shells as lemon curd would on its own. Pair this with lemon curd if desired. Pipe a ring of lemon buttercream on the macaron, then pipe the lemon curd in the middle (page 21). You may also use lemon juice and zest in place of lemon curd if desired.

Azuki Bean SMBC

250 g Swiss meringue buttercream
150 g Azuki bean paste
$\frac{1}{8}$ tsp salt

Place buttercream in a bowl and mix paste in gradually. Add salt. Spoon filling onto macarons using a teaspoon as beans may clog piping tip.

Chocolate SMBC

250 g Swiss meringue buttercream
80 g dark chocolate, chopped
  and melted

Place buttercream in a bowl and fold in melted dark chocolate.

Salted Caramel SMBC

200 g Swiss meringue buttercream
100 g salted caramel (page 32)

Place buttercream in a bowl and gradually mix in salted caramel.

Note: This cream offers a strong salted caramel flavour, whether plain, Earl Grey or spiced, while retaining a light texture that holds up well. Pair this with salted caramel if desired. Pipe a ring of salted caramel buttercream on the macaron, then pipe the salted caramel in the middle (page 21).

Salted Egg Yolk SMBC

250 g Swiss meringue buttercream
6 salted egg yolks (about 64 g)
2 Tbsp milk

Place buttercream in a bowl.

Steam salted egg yolks for 9 minutes and mash while hot. Add milk and mix well. Push through a wire mesh sieve to break up any lumps.

Gradually mix into buttercream.

Cookies & Cream SMBC

250 g Swiss meringue buttercream
70 g chocolate cream cookies,
   cream removed, cookies crushed

Cookies can be finely or coarsely crushed according to preference. Just keep in mind that larger pieces of cookies in cream will be harder to pipe.

Matcha SMBC

250 g Swiss meringue buttercream
1/2–1 Tbsp matcha powder

Place buttercream in a bowl and mix matcha in gradually, tasting as you go.

Note: You may want to make the flavour stronger and the cream a little more bitter as you are pairing it with sweet macaron shells.

Rose SMBC

250 g Swiss meringue buttercream

40 dried rosebuds

50 g hot milk

1 tsp beetroot powder or a little
  pink gel food colouring (optional)

Place buttercream in a bowl.

Steep rosebuds in hot milk for about
30 minutes. Strain milk and squeeze any
milk out of rosebuds. Colour with beetroot
powder or food colouring if desired.

Measure out 35 g rose-flavoured milk and
add to buttercream a teaspoonful at a time.

Note: Rose water may be used in place of
rosebuds. Add 1 Tbsp rose water to the
buttercream and whisk until well combined.

Lavender SMBC

250 g Swiss meringue buttercream

2$\frac{1}{2}$ tsp dried lavender flowers

50 g hot milk

A little blue gel food colouring (optional)

Place buttercream in a bowl.

Steep lavender flowers in hot milk for
about 30 minutes. Strain milk and squeeze
any milk out of flowers. Colour with food
colouring if desired.

Measure out 30 g lavender-flavoured milk
and add to buttercream one teaspoonful at
a time.

Tips on Making Flavoured SMBC

- Use a spatula, hand whisk or electric handheld mixer to mix in the flavouring.

- Add the flavouring gradually and taste as you go along to avoid adding too much flavouring.

- If using buttercream that has been frozen, bring it to room temperature and whisk to regain the right consistency before incorporating the flavouring.

- When using liquid-based flavouring, bear in mind that it will soften the Swiss meringue buttercream. Add a little at a time and check the consistency often to avoid the buttercream becoming too runny.

Non-Refrigerated Fillings

At times, it may be necessary to use fillings that do not require refrigeration especially when there is an outdoor event and the weather is hot and humid. Some possible options include peanut butter, melted dark chocolate and white chocolate-based fillings.

Just as Swiss meringue buttercream (SMBC) is my base of choice for making different flavours of refrigerated macaron fillings, white chocolate is my base of choice for non-refrigerated macaron fillings. The only issue I have with white chocolate is that it is on the sweet side, so I try to match it with ingredients such as tea or sour fruit that counter its sweetness. The recipes that follow have rather strong flavours, but they go well with the sweet macaron shells.

Lemon White Chocolate

200 g white chocolate, finely chopped

2 1/2 tsp lemon extract

1/2 tsp lemon paste

1 tsp finely grated lemon zest

35 g vegetable shortening

1/2 tsp salt

Yellow gel food colouring (optional)

Melt chocolate in a bowl set over a pot of simmering water. Alternatively, place in a microwave-safe bowl and heat in the microwave oven on Medium for 10 seconds and stir. Repeat until chocolate is melted and smooth.

Place lemon extract, lemon paste, lemon zest, shortening and salt in a small saucepan and cook over low heat until shortening is melted.

Gradually add lemon mixture to white chocolate, stirring well after each addition.

Add a little yellow food colouring if desired. Stir well.

Let mixture sit at room temperature for a few minutes to firm up a little before using. The filling should have the consistency of toothpaste.

Orange White Chocolate

200 g white chocolate, finely chopped

2 1/2 tsp orange extract

1/2 tsp orange paste

1 tsp finely grated orange zest

35 g vegetable shortening

1/2 tsp salt

Orange gel food colouring (optional)

Melt chocolate in a bowl set over a pot of simmering water. Alternatively, place in a microwave-safe bowl and heat in the microwave oven on Medium for 10 seconds and stir. Repeat until chocolate is melted and smooth.

Place orange extract, orange paste, orange zest, shortening and salt in a small saucepan and cook over low heat until shortening is melted.

Gradually add orange mixture to white chocolate, stirring well after each addition.

Add a little orange food colouring if desired. Stir well.

Let mixture sit at room temperature for a few minutes to firm up a little before using. The filling should have the consistency of toothpaste.

Earl Grey White Chocolate

200 g white chocolate, finely chopped

35 g vegetable shortening

1/2 tsp salt

5 tsp instant Earl Grey powder

Melt chocolate in a bowl set over a pot of simmering water. Alternatively, place in a microwave-safe bowl and heat in the microwave oven on Medium for 10 seconds and stir. Repeat until chocolate is melted and smooth.

Place shortening and salt in a small saucepan over low heat. Stir until shortening is melted.

Sift tea powder into melted chocolate and stir in a single direction until well combined.

Add melted shortening and stir until well combined.

Let mixture sit at room temperature for a few minutes to firm up a little before using. The filling should have the consistency of toothpaste.

Matcha White Chocolate

200 g white chocolate, finely chopped

35 g vegetable shortening

1/2 tsp salt

5 tsp matcha powder

Melt chocolate in a bowl set over a pot of simmering water. Alternatively, place in a microwave-safe bowl and heat in the microwave oven on Medium for 10 seconds and stir. Repeat until chocolate is melted and smooth.

Place shortening and salt in a small saucepan over low heat. Stir until shortening is melted.

Sift matcha powder into melted chocolate and stir in a single direction until well combined.

Add melted shortening and stir until well combined.

Let mixture sit at room temperature for a few minutes to firm up a little before using. The filling should have the consistency of toothpaste.

Strawberry White Chocolate

200 g white chocolate, finely chopped

35 g vegetable shortening

2½ tsp strawberry paste

1 tsp rose water (optional, but the flavour will be much better with this secret ingredient!)

½ tsp salt

Melt chocolate in a bowl set over a pot of simmering water. Alternatively, place in a microwave-safe bowl and heat in the microwave oven on Medium for 10 seconds and stir. Repeat until chocolate is melted and smooth.

Place shortening, strawberry paste, rose water and salt in a small saucepan over low heat. Stir until shortening is melted.

Gradually add melted shortening to melted chocolate, stirring well after each addition.

Let mixture sit at room temperature for a few minutes to firm up a little before using. The filling should have the consistency of toothpaste.

Frequently Asked Questions

Age Egg Whites

Do I need to age the egg whites used in making the meringue?

There has been a lot of discussion among bakers about the necessity of ageing egg whites when making macarons. Egg whites are aged to reduce the level of moisture in the batter, but this is not necessary although I find that it saves time to separate the eggs in advance.

Process Almond Powder

Do I need to process the almond powder before sifting?

If the almond powder you are using is not superfine, you may need to process it to make it easier to sift and ensure that the macarons have a smoother finish. Alternatively, sift more almond powder than what the recipe calls for to obtain the amount needed and discard the larger bits that do not pass through the sieve.

Use Cream of Tartar

Do I need to add cream of tartar when beating the egg whites to increase the stability of the Italian meringue?

I find it unnecessary to add cream of tartar although some bakers use it. In these recipes, I use Italian meringue which is rather stable by nature as the egg whites are partially cooked in the process.

Prepare Italian Meringue

How do you beat the egg whites with a handheld mixer and prepare the syrup for the Italian meringue at the same time?

Before I got a stand mixer, I suspended the candy thermometer over the pot of boiling syrup with a pair of tongs while whisking the egg whites with a hand whisk until the soft peak stage. Once the syrup reached 115°C, I switched to a handheld mixer. Use a heavy metal bowl for whipping the meringue so it doesn't spin around as you pour the syrup with one hand and operate the handheld mixer with the other!

Reduce Sugar

Can I reduce the amount of sugar in the recipe?

Sugar is used to give the shells structure and shape. Reducing the amount of sugar will compromise the structural stability of the shells. Choose savoury (e.g. salted caramel or salted egg yolk), sour (e.g. lemon) or bitter (e.g. dark chocolate or matcha) fillings to offset the sweetness of the shells.

Store Macaron Batter

Can I store unused macaron batter?

Macarons are best baked from freshly prepared batter, but should there be any batter left over, wrap it tightly with plastic wrap. Make sure that there are no air pockets between the batter and the wrap and store it in the fridge for no more than a day. I have tried baking macarons with day-old batter and they turned out as usual.

Pipe Without Piping Tip

Can I cut a hole in the piping bag instead of using a round piping tip to pipe the macaron batter?

You may do this if you are piping very simple shapes and you are not particular about the macarons turning up slightly differently from shell to shell. Macarons with complex shapes require precise tip sizes for the final product to turn out well.

Shells Browned But Wet Inside

My shells have browned on the outside, but are still wet inside. What should I do?

Your oven temperature could be set too high. Use an oven thermometer to check the temperature of your oven to ensure the temperature setting is accurate. You can also try placing the baking tray on the lowest rack in the oven or turning the temperature down and baking for a longer time after the initial 16–20 minutes.

Skip Resting Piped Macarons

Can I skip resting the piped macaron shells before baking?

Resting the piped batter allows a thin membrane to form on the surface. This will help prevent the shells from cracking during baking (see page 21) and ensures the formation of the macaron "feet" which are the ruffles on the edges of the shell. If you are pressed for time, speed up the process by placing the piped macarons in an air-conditioned room or blowing a fan at the shells.

Hollow Macaron Shells

Why are my macaron shells hollow?

There are a few possibilities. You did not beat enough air out of the macaron batter, the batter was over mixed, the Italian meringue was under- or over-beaten, or the oven temperature was too low.

Use the fold and press technique (page 18) when mixing the macaron batter to knock some air out of the Italian meringue. The Italian meringue should be shiny and smooth, and be able to hold a peak that may curl a little when the beater is lifted slowly. Broken or lumpy meringue is over beaten, whereas an under beaten meringue is unable to hold a peak.

Do not skip the "press" motion when mixing the macaron batter. Do not over mix or the batter will become runny. Test the consistency of the batter often.

Pipe Fancy Shapes

How do you pipe such fancy macarons?

The aim of this book is precisely to answer this question! Use templates! Place your chosen template (provided at the back of this book) on the baking tray. Place a sheet of baking paper over it and pipe away! Do not fill the template all the way to the edge as the batter will spread a little after piping. You should also take care not to overmix the batter to ensure that the batter will hold its shape after piping.

Finally, practise makes perfect!

Bake Multiple Trays

Can I bake two trays at a time on different racks in the oven to speed things up?

I would not recommend it unless you have a commercial oven as macarons are sensitive to baking temperature. If using a home oven, the shells on the upper tray may brown too much if the temperature is higher, and the shells on the lower tray may end up being hollow if the temperature is lower. You may switch the position of the trays halfway through baking and see if it works, but it will be a risk as the actual temperature on each rack is hard to control for home bakers.

Template Burn During Baking

Will the paper template under the baking paper burn during baking?

Printing paper for home/office inkjet printers are able to withstand baking temperatures without burning. I have not had a single incident of the paper template burning in the oven.

Design Templates

How do you design macaron templates?

You can search for soft copies of images that you like or do your own drawings on paper and scan them. Once you have your image, use an edge detection function of an imaging software to help you obtain a line drawing of the image. You can then copy the line drawing image into a Word document and resize it. Macarons typically measure 4–6 cm, so resize the image according to your preferred size. Copy and paste the image several times on the Word document for half the shells, and fill the other half of the document with a mirror image of the original line drawing if the image is not symmetrical. Keep each image at least 1 cm apart or have a wider margin between shells if you are new to baking macarons.

Consume Immediately After Filling

Can I consume filled macarons immediately?

You may, but macarons taste better after being left to mature for 1–3 days. During this time, the shells will absorb moisture and flavour from the filling and soften slightly.

Portion Mass and Meringue

If I have to prepare several colours of batter for a batch of macarons, how do I portion the mass and Italian meringue accurately?

Prepare a batch of uncoloured mass and divide it into portions for the different colours. You may portion out the mass based on the estimated area that each colour covers for your subject. Use the ratio of 0.55 for weight of Italian meringue/weight of mass to portion the Italian meringue. You will end up with a little excess meringue which you may use to stick the baking paper onto the baking tray.

My Favourite Things

Colourful Balloons Macaron Pops

Makes 50–60 macarons

  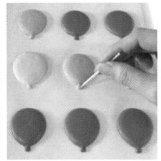 

Mass

210 g almond powder

210 g icing sugar

84 g egg whites, divided into
3 portions, each 28 g

Colouring for Mass

5 g red yeast powder (optional)

5 g natural yellow powder
(optional)

2 g beetroot powder (optional)

1 tsp dried blue pea flowers
(optional)

Red, blue and golden yellow
gel food colouring

Italian Meringue

84 g egg whites,
at room temperature

210 g sugar

78 g water

Suggested Filling

You may choose flavours
to match the colour of the
balloons, such as strawberry
SMBC (page 34) for red
balloons, lavender SMBC
(page 36) for blue balloons
and lemon SMBC (page 34)
with lemon curd (page 31)
for yellow balloons.

1. Prepare baking tray and balloon template (page 116).

2. Prepare mass. Sift together almond powder and icing sugar.
   Mix well. Divide into 3 equal portions. Sift red yeast powder
   into one portion and natural yellow powder into another,
   if using. Mix well.

3. Colour egg whites for mass. Mix beetroot powder into a portion
   of egg whites. Place blue pea flowers into another portion of
   egg whites and let steep (page 27), if using.

4. Add coloured egg whites to respective coloured almond
   mixture and mix well. Add a little gel food colouring until
   desired shade is obtained.

5. Prepare Italian meringue (page 16). Divide into 3 equal portions.

6. Prepare macaron batter (page 18). Fold a portion of meringue
   into each mass.

7. Spoon 1 Tbsp of each batter into individual piping bags each
   fitted with a 3-mm round tip. Spoon remaining batters into
   individual piping bags each fitted with a 6-mm round tip.

8. Using larger tips, pipe ovals onto baking tray using template
   as a guide. Tap tray to release trapped air bubbles. Set aside
   for 15 minutes or until a thin membrane forms.

9. Using smaller tips, pipe a small dollop of batter at the base
   of each oval. Use a toothpick to pull batter into desired shape.

10. Let shells dry (page 20).

11. Bake in a preheated oven at 135°C for 17–20 minutes with tray
    on bottom rack. Rotate tray halfway through baking. Let shells
    cool on tray before removing.

12. Prepare filling. Pipe filling on bottom shells and place a cake
    pop stick in the middle. Top with more filling to cover stick and
    place top shell over.

13. Store in an airtight container and refrigerate for at least
    24 hours before serving.

Teacup Macarons

Makes 40–50 macarons

Mass

200 g almond powder

200 g icing sugar or lavender
icing sugar (see Note)

1 Tbsp dried blue pea flowers
(optional)

80 g egg whites,
at room temperature

Sky blue and royal blue
gel food colouring

Italian Meringue

80 g egg whites,
at room temperature

200 g sugar

75 g water

Finishing

Pink royal icing (page 29)

> **Suggested Filling**
>
> Lavender SMBC (page 36)

Note: To make lavender icing
sugar, place 2 Tbsp dried
lavender flowers in an airtight jar
with 250 g icing sugar. Set aside
for at least a week before using.

1. Prepare baking tray and teacup template (page 117).

2. Prepare mass. Sift together almond powder and icing sugar. Mix well.

3. Place blue pea flowers into egg whites for mass and let steep (page 27), if using.

4. Add blue coloured egg whites to almond mixture and mix well. Add a little gel food colouring until desired shade is reached. Mix well.

5. Prepare Italian meringue (page 16).

6. Prepare macaron batter (page 18). Fold meringue into mass.

7. Spoon 2 Tbsp batter into a piping bag fitted with a 3-mm round tip and remainder into a piping bag fitted with a 6-mm round tip.

8. Using larger tip, pipe body of teacup onto baking tray using template as a guide. Tap tray to release trapped air bubbles. Set aside for 15 minutes or until a thin membrane forms.

9. Using smaller tip, pipe base and handle of teacups onto top shells.

10. Let shells dry (page 20).

11. Bake in a preheated oven at 135°C for 17–20 minutes with tray on bottom rack. Rotate tray halfway through baking. Let shells cool on tray before removing.

12. Prepare some pink royal icing. Spoon royal icing into a piping bag fitted with a 2-mm piping tip and outline rim of teacups. Set aside to dry for an hour.

13. Prepare filling. Sandwich shells with filling. Store in an airtight container and refrigerate for at least 24 hours before serving.

Colour Pencil Macarons

Makes 40–50 macarons

Mass

200 g almond powder

200 g icing sugar

80 g egg whites,
    at room temperature

Blue, red and orange gel or
    powdered food colouring

Italian Meringue

80 g egg whites,
    at room temperature

200 g sugar

75 g water

Suggested Filling

Orange white
chocolate (page 39)

1. Prepare baking tray and pencil template (page 117).

2. Prepare mass. Sift together almond powder and icing sugar. Mix well. Add egg whites for mass and mix well.

3. Divide mass into 3 equal portions. Colour one portion blue, another red and the third orange. If using powdered colouring, sift powder over mass before mixing it in. Colour orange mass lightly to mimic colour of wooden pencils.

4. Prepare Italian meringue (page 16). Divide into 3 equal portions.

5. Prepare macaron batter (page 18). Fold a portion of meringue into each mass.

6. Spoon 1 Tbsp each of blue and red batters into individual piping bags each fitted with a 2-mm round tip. Spoon remaining blue and red batters into individual piping bags each fitted with a 6-mm round tip. Spoon orange batter into a piping bag fitted with a 4-mm round tip.

7. Using larger tips, pipe blue and red rectangles onto baking tray with pencil template as a guide. Pipe triangles using orange batter.

8. Using smaller tips, pipe a small dollop of blue or red batter at tip of triangles. Use a toothpick to pull batter into desired shape. Tap tray to release trapped air bubbles.

9. Let shells dry (page 20).

10. Bake in a preheated oven at 135°C for 17–20 minutes with tray on bottom rack. Rotate tray halfway through baking. Let shells cool on tray before removing.

11. Prepare filling of choice. Sandwich shells with filling. Store in an airtight container for at least 24 hours before serving.

Pretty Clothing Macarons

Makes 45–55 macarons

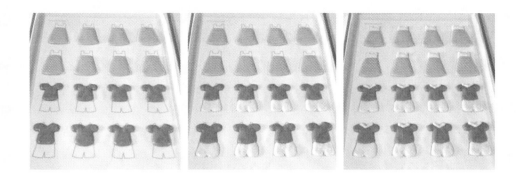

Mass

210 g almond powder

210 g icing sugar

4 g natural pink powder
    and/or pink gel food colouring

4 g matcha powder

1/4 tsp white powder food colouring
    (optional)

84 g egg whites, divided into
    3 portions, each 28 g

Italian Meringue

84 g egg whites, at room
    temperature

210 g sugar

78 g water

Finishing

White and pink royal icing (page 29)

Suggested Filling

Azuki bean SMBC (page
34) and/or matcha SMBC
(page 35)

1. Prepare baking tray and clothing template (page 118).

2. Prepare mass. Sift together almond powder and icing sugar. Mix well. Divide into 3 equal portions.

3. Sift natural pink powder into one portion, matcha powder into another and white powder into the third portion if using. Mix well. Add 28 g egg whites to each portion and mix well.

4. Add a few drops of pink gel food colouring to pink mass if a darker shade of pink is preferred.

5. Prepare Italian meringue (page 16). Divide into 3 equal portions.

6. Prepare macaron batter (page 18). Fold a portion of meringue into each mass.

7. Spoon 2 Tbsp white batter into a piping bag fitted with a 3-mm round tip. Spoon remaining white batter, and pink and green batters into individual piping bags each fitted with a 6-mm round tip.

8. Pipe skirts with pink batter and shirts with green batter using template as a guide. Tap tray to release trapped air bubbles.

9. Using white batter with larger tip, pipe shorts and bodice of dress using template as a guide.

10. Using white batter with smaller tip, pipe dress straps and shirt collar. Tap tray to release trapped air bubbles.

11. Let shells dry (page 20).

12. Bake in a preheated oven at 135°C for 17–20 minutes with tray on bottom rack. Rotate tray halfway through baking. Let shells cool on tray before removing.

13. Prepare some white and pink royal icing. Spoon into individual piping bags each fitted with a 1-mm round tip. Pipe details on top shells. Set aside to dry for an hour.

14. Prepare filling. Sandwich shells with filling. Store in an airtight container and refrigerate for at least 24 hours before serving.

Strawberry Ice Cream Cone Macarons

Makes 45–55 macarons

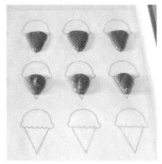   

Mass

200 g almond powder

200 g icing sugar

5 g natural pink powder (optional)

5 g cocoa powder

80 g egg whites, at room temperature divided into 2 portions, each 40 g

1/8 tsp strawberry paste (optional)

Pink gel food colouring

Italian Meringue

80 g egg whites, at room temperature

200 g sugar

75 g water

Finishing

Rainbow sprinkles

Brown royal icing (page 29)

> ### Suggested Filling
> Strawberry SMBC (page 34)

1. Prepare baking tray and ice cream cone template (page 118).

2. Prepare mass. Sift together almond powder and icing sugar. Mix well. Divide into 2 equal portions. Sift natural pink powder into one portion and cocoa powder into the other. Mix well.

3. Add 40 g egg whites into each portion and mix well.

4. Add strawberry paste and pink gel food colouring to pink portion if using and mix well.

5. Prepare Italian meringue (page 16). Divide into 2 equal portions.

6. Prepare macaron batter (page 18). Fold a portion of meringue into each mass.

7. Spoon pink and brown batters into individual piping bags each fitted with a 5-mm round tip.

8. Pipe ice cream cones with brown batter using template as a guide. Use a toothpick to pull batter into desired shape.

9. Pipe ice cream with pink batter using template as a guide. Begin by piping an oval for scoop of ice cream, leaving a gap between ice cream and cone. Next, pipe a few small circles to cover gap.

10. Tap tray to release trapped air bubbles. Sprinkle rainbow sprinkles on pink portion.

11. Let shells dry (page 20).

12. Bake in a preheated oven at 135°C for 17–20 minutes with tray on bottom rack. Rotate tray halfway through baking. Let shells cool on tray before removing.

13. Prepare some brown royal icing. Spoon into a piping bag fitted with a 1-mm round tip. Pipe criss-cross lines on cone. Set aside to dry for an hour.

14. Prepare filling. Sandwich shells with filling. Store in an airtight container and refrigerate for at least 24 hours before serving.

Frosted Cupcake Macarons

Makes 40–50 macarons

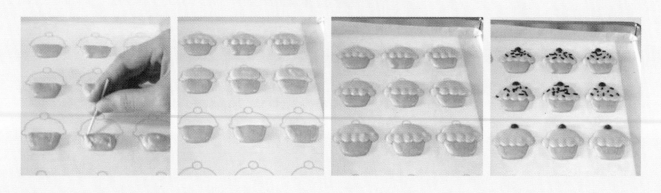

Mass

200 g almond powder

200 g icing sugar

80 g egg whites, at room
temperature divided into
2 portions, each 40 g

5 g natural pink powder (optional)

1/8 tsp strawberry paste or
raspberry extract (optional)

Pink, teal and red
gel food colouring

Italian Meringue

80 g egg whites, at room
temperature

200 g sugar

75 g water

Finishing

Chocolate rice

White royal icing (page 29)

Suggested Filling

Strawberry SMBC (page 34)
with chocolate ganache
(page 31) centre

1. Prepare baking trays and cupcake template (page 119).

2. Prepare mass. Sift together almond powder and icing sugar. Mix well. Divide into 2 equal portions. Sift natural pink powder into one portion and mix well. Add 40 g egg whites to each portion and mix well.

3. Add strawberry paste/raspberry extract and a few drops of pink gel food colouring to pink portion if a darker shade of pink is preferred. Mix well. Add a few drops of teal gel food colouring to other portion. Mix well.

4. Prepare Italian meringue (page 16). Divide into 2 equal portions.

5. Prepare macaron batter (page 18). Fold a portion of meringue into each mass. Fold pink batter until only some streaks of meringue are still visible. Spoon 2 Tbsp pink batter into a small bowl, add a drop of red gel food colouring and fold until well combined. Fold remaining pink and teal batters until no trace of meringue is visible.

6. Spoon pink and teal batters into individual piping bags each fitted with a 6-mm round tip. Spoon red batter into a piping bag fitted with a 3-mm round tip.

7. Pipe cupcake cases with teal batter using template as a guide. Use a toothpick to pull batter into desired shape.

8. Pipe cake with pink batter using template as a guide. Begin by piping an oval for cake, leaving a gap between cake and cupcake case. Next, pipe a few small circles to cover gap.

9. Tap tray to release trapped air bubbles. Sprinkle chocolate rice on pink portion. Set aside for 15 minutes or until a thin membrane forms.

10. Pipe a red circle on top of each cupcake for cherry with red batter. Tap tray again.

11. Let shells dry (page 20).

12. Bake in a preheated oven at 135°C for 17–20 minutes with tray on bottom rack. Rotate tray halfway through baking. Let shells cool on tray before removing.

13. Prepare some white royal icing. Spoon into a piping bag fitted with 1-mm round tip. Pipe lines on cupcake cases. Set aside to dry for an hour.

14. Prepare filling. Pipe a ring of strawberry SMBC on bottom shells and fill centre with chocolate ganache. Sandwich with top shells. Store in an airtight container and refrigerate for at least 24 hours before serving.

Watermelon Wedges Macarons

Makes 45–55 macarons

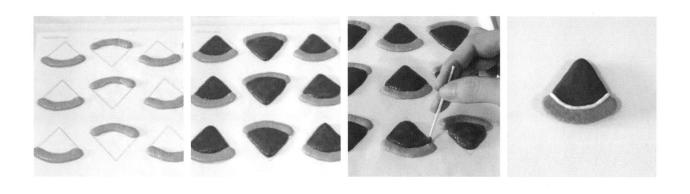

Mass

200 g almond powder

200 g icing sugar

80 g egg whites, at room temperature, divided into 60 g and 20 g portions

Colouring for Mass

5 g red yeast powder (optional)

3 g matcha powder

3 g beetroot powder (optional)

$1/8$ tsp strawberry emulco (optional)

Red gel food colouring

Italian Meringue

80 g egg whites, at room temperature

200 g sugar

75 g water

Finishing

White royal icing (page 29)

Black edible ink marker

Suggested Filling
Strawberry white chocolate (page 41)

1. Prepare baking tray and watermelon template (page 119).

2. Prepare mass. Sift together almond powder and icing sugar. Mix well. Divide almond mixture into a 300 g and 100 g portion. Sift red yeast powder into 300 g portion, if using, and matcha powder into 100 g portion. Mix well.

3. Dissolve beetroot powder into 60 g egg whites, if using. Add to red almond mixture together with strawberry emulco and a few drops of red gel food colouring. Mix well. Adjust to desired shade.

4. Add 20 g egg whites to green almond mixture. Mix well.

5. Prepare Italian meringue (page 16).

6. Prepare macaron batter (page 18). Fold three-quarters of meringue into red mass. Fold remaining meringue into green mass.

7. Spoon red and green batters into individual piping bags each fitted with a 6-mm round tip.

8. Pipe an arc with green batter for watermelon rind using template as a guide. Pipe a red triangle for watermelon flesh. Use a toothpick to pull batter into desired shape. Tap tray to release trapped air bubbles.

9. Let shells dry (page 20).

10. Bake in a preheated oven at 140°C for 16–20 minutes with tray on bottom rack. Rotate tray halfway through baking. Let shells cool on tray before removing.

11. Prepare some white royal icing. Spoon into a piping bag fitted with 1-mm round tip. Pipe white of watermelon rind. Set aside to dry for an hour.

12. Use a black edible ink marker to draw watermelon seeds.

13. Prepare filling. Sandwich shells with filling. Store in an airtight container for at least 24 hours before serving.

Juicy Carrot Macarons

Makes 40–50 macarons

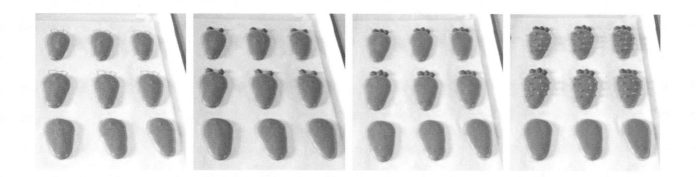

Mass

200 g almond powder

200 g icing sugar

15 g carrot powder

Orange and green gel food colouring

80 g egg whites, at room temperature, divided into 70 g and 10 g portions

Italian Meringue

80 g egg whites, at room temperature

200 g sugar

75 g water

Suggested Filling

Spiced salted caramel SMBC (page 35)

---

1. Prepare baking tray and carrot template (page 121).

2. Prepare mass. Sift together almond powder and icing sugar. Mix well. Divide almond mixture into 350 g and 50 g portions.

3. Sift carrot powder into 350 g almond mixture. Mix well. Add 70 g egg whites and mix again. Adjust colour with orange gel food colouring if desired.

4. Add 10 g egg whites and a few drops of green gel food colouring to 50 g almond mixture. Mix well.

5. Prepare Italian meringue (page 16).

6. Prepare macaron batter (page 18). Fold one-eight of meringue into green mass. Fold remainder into orange mass.

7. Spoon 1 Tbsp orange batter into a piping bag fitted with a 1-mm round tip and remainder into a piping bag fitted with a 6-mm round tip. Spoon green batter into a piping bag fitted with a 3-mm round tip.

8. Using orange batter with larger tip, pipe long triangles for carrots using template as a guide. Tap tray to release trapped air bubbles.

9. Pipe leaves with green batter using template as a guide. Do this only for top shells. Begin by piping 2 short lines on top end of carrot, leaving a gap in the middle. Set aside for 15 minutes or until a thin membrane forms. Pipe middle leaf.

10. Using orange batter with smaller tip, pipe lines on carrots.

11. Let shells dry (page 20).

12. Bake in a preheated oven at 135°C for 17–20 minutes with tray on bottom rack. Rotate tray halfway through baking. Let shells cool on tray before removing.

13. Prepare filling. Sandwich shells with filling. Store in an airtight container and refrigerate for at least 24 hours before serving.

Around Town

Traffic Light Macaron Pops

Makes 16–20 macarons pops

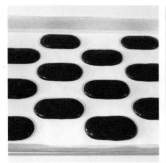   

Mass

210 g almond powder

210 g icing sugar

84 g egg whites, at room
temperature, divided into
56 g and 28 g portions

1¹/₂ tsp cocoa powder

10 g charcoal powder

¹/₄ tsp vanilla bean paste (optional)

Black, red, yellow and green
gel food colouring

Italian Meringue

84 g egg whites, at room
temperature

210 g sugar

78 g water

Suggested Filling

Melted dark/milk chocolate
and/or peanut butter

---

1. Prepare baking trays and traffic light templates (page 120).

2. Prepare mass. Sift together almond powder and icing sugar. Mix well. Divide almond mixture into 280 g and 140 g portions.

3. Sift cocoa and charcoal powders into 280 g portion. Mix well. Add 56 g egg whites, vanilla bean paste and a few drops of black food colouring Mix well.

4. Add 28 g egg whites to 140 g portion. Mix well. Divide mass into 3 equal portions and colour them red, yellow and green with gel food colouring. Mix well.

5. Prepare Italian meringue (page 16).

6. Prepare macaron batter (page 18). Fold two-thirds of meringue into black mass. Divide remaining meringue into 3 portions and fold a portion each into red, yellow and green masses.

7. Spoon black batter into a piping bag fitted with a 6-mm round tip. Spoon red, yellow and green batters into individual piping bags each fitted with a 5-mm round tip.

8. Pipe black oblongs for traffic light box using template as a guide. On separate tray, pipe circles for lights using red, yellow and green batter using template as a guide. Tap trays to release trapped air bubbles.

9. Let shells dry (page 20).

10. Bake black shells in a preheated oven at 140°C for 20–25 minutes with tray on second lowest rack and round shells at 135°C for 13–16 minutes with tray on bottom rack. Rotate tray halfway through baking. Let shells cool on tray before removing.

11. Piped chocolate/peanut butter on half of traffic light box shells. Place an ice cream stick in the middle. Top with more filling to cover stick and sandwich with other shell. Stick coloured circles on traffic light boxes using chocolate/peanut butter.

12. Store in an airtight container for at least 24 hours before serving.

Speedy Car Macarons

Makes 40–50 macarons

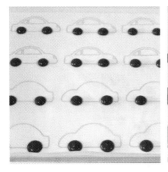   

Mass

200 g almond powder

200 g icing sugar

80 g egg whites, at room temperature, divided into 60 g and 20 g portions

Colouring for Mass

5 g red yeast powder (optional)

5 g charcoal powder

3 g beetroot powder (optional)

1/8 tsp strawberry emulco

Red and black gel food colouring

Italian Meringue

80 g egg whites, at room temperature

200 g sugar

75 g water

Finishing

Light blue, grey and orange/yellow royal icing (page 29)

Suggested Filling

Strawberry SMBC (page 34)

1. Prepare baking tray and car template (page 121).

2. Prepare mass. Sift together almond powder and icing sugar. Mix well. Divide almond mixture into 300 g and 100 g portions.

3. Sift red yeast powder into 300 g portion if using. Mix well. Sift charcoal powder into 100 g portion. Mix well.

4. Dissolve beetroot powder into 60 g egg whites if using. Add to red almond mixture with strawberry emulco and a few drops of red gel food colouring to obtain desired shade.

5. Add 20 g egg whites and a few drops of black gel food colouring to black almond mixture to obtain desired shade. Mix well.

6. Prepare Italian meringue (page 16).

7. Prepare macaron batter (page 18). Fold three-quarters of meringue into red mass and remaining meringue into black mass.

8. Spoon batters into individual piping bags each fitted with a 4-mm round tip. Pipe wheels with black batter using template as a guide. Tap tray to release trapped air bubbles.

9. Pipe car body with red batter using template as a guide. Begin by tracing outline of car, then filling with batter. Use a toothpick to pull batter into corners and around wheels. Tap tray to release trapped air bubbles.

10. Let shells dry (page 20).

11. Bake in a preheated oven at 140°C for 16–20 minutes with tray on bottom rack. Rotate tray halfway through baking. Let shells cool on tray before removing.

12. Prepare some light blue, grey and orange/yellow royal icing. Spoon into individual piping bags each fitted with a 1-mm round tip. Pipe windows, rims and headlights. Use a toothpick to pull icing into edges. Do this only for top shells. Set aside to dry for 1–3 hours.

13. Prepare filling. Sandwich shells with filling. Store in an airtight container and refrigerate for at least 24 hours before serving.

Choo-choo Train Macarons

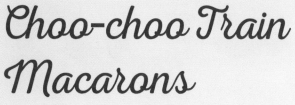

Makes 35–45 macarons

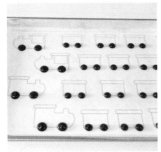   

Mass

200 g almond powder

200 g icing sugar

80 g egg whites, at room temperature

Colouring for Mass

Blue, red, green and black gel food colouring

5 g charcoal powder

Italian Meringue

80 g egg whites, at room temperature

200 g sugar

75 g water

Finishing

Yellow royal icing (page 29)

Suggested Filling

Dark chocolate ganache (page 31) or chocolate SMBC (page 34)

Note: To keep this recipe simple, I used only gel food colouring. You may choose to use natural food colouring to reduce the use of artificial colouring if preferred.

1. Prepare baking tray and train template (page 122) .

2. Prepare mass. Sift together almond powder and icing sugar. Mix well. Add egg whites and mix well.

3. Spoon one-third of mass into a bowl and add a few drops of blue gel food colouring. Mix well. Divide remaining mass into 3 equal portions and add a few drops of red gel food colouring to one portion and green to another. Mix well. Add charcoal powder to remaining portion and mix well, then add a few drops of black gel food colouring to obtain a darker shade if preferred.

4. Prepare Italian meringue (page 16). Portion out meringue for each colour using the formula: weight of meringue = 0.55 x weight of mass.

5. Prepare macaron batter (page 18). Fold respective meringue into each mass.

6. Spoon batters into individual piping bags each fitted with a 4-mm round tip. Pipe circles for wheels with black batter using template as a guide. Tap tray to release trapped air bubbles.

7. Pipe locomotive and carriages by tracing outline of parts, then filling with batter. Use a toothpick to pull batter into corners and around wheels. Tap tray to release trapped air bubbles.

8. Let shells dry (page 20).

9. Bake in a preheated oven at 140°C for 16–20 minutes with tray on bottom rack. Rotate tray halfway through baking. Let shells cool on tray before removing.

10. Prepare some yellow royal icing. Spoon into a piping bag fitted with a 1-mm tip. Pipe windows, rims and headlights. Use a toothpick to pull icing into edges. Set aside to dry for 1–3 hours.

11. Prepare filling. Sandwich shells with filling. Store in an airtight container and refrigerate for at least 24 hours before serving.

Cruise Ship Macarons

Makes 40–50 macarons

Mass

200 g almond powder

200 g icing sugar

80 g egg whites, at room temperature

Blue, red, yellow and white gel food colouring

Italian Meringue

80 g egg whites, at room temperature

200 g sugar

75 g water

Finishing

Blue royal icing (page 29)

Suggested Filling

Dark chocolate ganache (page 31) or chocolate SMBC (page 34)

Note: To keep this recipe simple, I used only gel food colouring. You may choose to use natural food colouring to reduce the use of artificial colouring if preferred.

1. Prepare baking tray and ship template (page 122).

2. Prepare mass. Sift together almond powder and icing sugar. Mix well. Add egg whites and mix well. Divide mass into 3 equal portions.

3. Add a few drops of blue gel food colouring to one portion and red to another. Mix well.

4. Divide third portion into 2 equal parts. Add a few drops of yellow gel food colouring to one portion and white to the other. Mix well.

5. Prepare Italian meringue (page 16). Divide into 3 equal portions.

6. Prepare macaron batter (page 18). Fold one-third of meringue into blue mass and another into red mass. Divide third portion of meringue into 2 and fold one into yellow mass and the other into white mass.

7. Spoon batters into individual piping bags each fitted with a 4-mm round tip. Begin by piping roof of cabin with yellow batter using template as a guide.

8. Pipe side of ship and chimney with red batter. Use a toothpick to pull batter into corners. Tap tray to release trapped air bubbles.

9. Pipe cabin using white batter and hull with blue batter. Use a toothpick to pull batter into corners. Tap tray to release trapped air bubbles.

10. Let shells dry (page 20).

11. Bake in a preheated oven at 135°C for 17–20 minutes with tray on bottom rack. Rotate tray halfway through baking. Let shells cool on tray before removing.

12. Prepare some blue royal icing. Spoon into a piping bag fitted with a 1-mm tip. Pipe details on ship. Set aside to dry for 1 hour.

13. Prepare filling. Sandwich shells with filling. Store in an airtight container and refrigerate for at least 24 hours before serving.

Aircraft Macarons

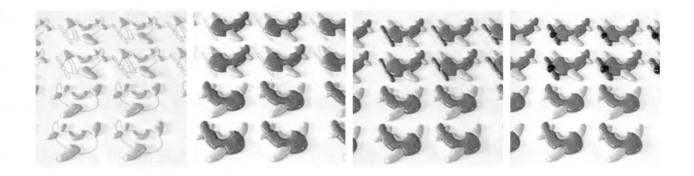

Mass

200 g almond powder

200 g icing sugar

80 g egg whites, at room temperature, divided into 2 portions

Colouring for Mass

$^{1}/_{2}$ Tbsp dried blue pea flowers (optional)

5 g natural yellow powder (optional)

Blue and yellow gel food colouring

Charcoal powder

Italian Meringue

80 g egg whites, at room temperature

200 g sugar

75 g water

Finishing

Pale blue royal icing (page 29)

Suggested Filling

Dark chocolate ganache (page 31) or melted dark chocolate

1. Prepare baking tray and aircraft template (page 123).

2. Prepare mass. Sift together almond powder and icing sugar. Mix well. Divide into 2 equal portions. Sift yellow powder into one portion, if using. Mix well. Place blue pea flowers into a portion of egg whites and let steep (page 27), if using.

3. Add blue egg whites to plain almond mixture. Mix well. Add plain egg whites to yellow mass. Mix well. Add a little gel food colouring to each mass to obtain desired shade.

4. Prepare Italian meringue (page 16). Divide into 2 equal portions.

5. Prepare macaron batter (page 18). Fold meringue into each mass.

6. Prepare grey and black batters. Spoon $1^{1}/_{2}$ Tbsp yellow batter into a small bowl. Gradually add charcoal powder a pinch at a time and until batter is black. Spoon 3 Tbsp blue batter into another bowl. Repeat to add charcoal until batter is grey. Spoon batters into individual piping bags each fitted with a 3-mm round tip.

7. Spoon yellow batter into a piping bag fitted with a 3-mm round tip and blue batter into a piping bag fitted with a 4-mm round tip.

8. Pipe cockpit and wings with yellow batter using template as a guide. Begin by tracing shape, then filling with batter. Use a toothpick to pull batter into desired shape. Pipe body of aircraft with blue batter. Pipe propellers only for top shells using grey and black batters. Tap tray to release trapped air bubbles.

9. Let shells dry (page 20).

10. Bake in a preheated oven at 135°C for 17–20 minutes with tray on bottom rack. Rotate tray halfway through baking. Let shells cool on tray before removing.

11. Prepare some pale blue royal icing. Spoon into a piping bag fitted with a 1-mm round tip and pipe details on aircraft. Do this only for top shells. Set aside to dry for 1 hour.

12. Prepare filling. Sandwich shells with filling. Store in an airtight container and refrigerate for at least 24 hours before serving.

Animal Friends

Galloping Horse Macarons

Makes 40–50 macarons

Mass

200 g almond powder

200 g icing sugar

80 g egg whites, at room temperature

Pink, white (optional), blue and purple gel food colouring

Italian Meringue

80 g egg whites, at room temperature

200 g sugar

75 g water

Finishing

Black edible ink marker

Suggested Filling

Rose SMBC (page 36)

1. Prepare baking tray and horse template (page 123).

2. Prepare mass. Sift together almond powder and icing sugar. Mix well. Add egg whites and mix well.

3. Spoon a quarter of mass into another bowl. Add a drop of pink gel food colouring and mix well. Leave larger portion plain or add a few drops of white gel food colouring and mix well.

4. Prepare Italian meringue (page 16).

5. Prepare macaron batter (page 18). Fold a quarter of meringue into pink mass and remaining meringue into white mass.

6. Spoon 2 Tbsp pink batter in a small bowl. Add a little blue and purple gel food colouring and mix well to get a purplish colour.

7. Spoon 1 Tbsp white batter into a piping bag fitted with a 3-mm round tip and remainder into a piping bag fitted with a 4-mm round tip. Spoon pink and purple batters into separate piping bags fitted with 3-mm round tips.

8. Using white batter with 4-mm tip, pipe outline of horse onto baking tray using template as a guide, then fill in centres. Pipe a small dollop of batter for ears with 3-mm tip, then use a toothpick to pull batter into shape. Tap tray to release trapped air bubbles. Set aside for 15 minutes or until a thin membrane forms.

9. Pipe mane with pink batter and use a toothpick to pull batter into shape. Repeat to pipe saddle using purple batter. Do this only for top shells.

10. Let shells dry (page 20).

11. Bake in a preheated oven at 130°C for 17–22 minutes with tray on bottom rack. Rotate tray halfway through baking. Let shells cool on tray before removing.

12. Use a black edible ink marker to draw horse's eye.

13. Prepare filling. Sandwich shells with filling. Store in an airtight container and refrigerate for at least 24 hours before serving.

Happy Elephant Macarons

Makes 35–45 macarons

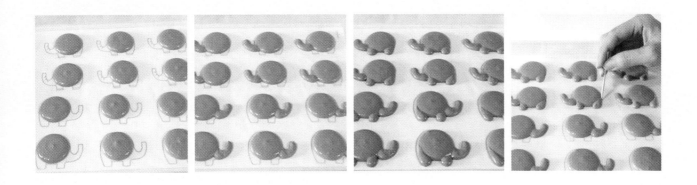

Mass

200 g almond powder

200 g icing sugar

1 tsp charcoal powder

½ tsp instant Earl Grey powder (optional)

80 g egg whites, at room temperature

Italian Meringue

80 g egg whites, at room temperature

200 g sugar

75 g water

Finishing

Black edible ink marker

Suggested Filling

Earl Grey white chocolate (page 40)

---

1. Prepare baking tray and elephant template (page 124).

2. Prepare mass. Sift together almond powder, icing sugar, charcoal powder and Earl Grey powder. Mix well. Add egg whites and mix well.

3. Prepare Italian meringue (page 16).

4. Prepare macaron batter (page 18). Fold meringue into mass.

5. Spoon batter into a piping bag fitted with a 6-mm round tip.

6. Pipe circles for elephants using template as a guide. Pipe curved line for trunk. Pipe short lines for legs, then use a toothpick to pull batter into shape. Tap tray to release trapped air bubbles.

7. Let shells dry (page 20).

8. Bake in a preheated oven at 135°C for 17–20 minutes with tray on bottom rack. Rotate tray halfway through baking. Let shells cool on tray before removing.

9. Use a black edible ink marker to draw details on elephant.

10. Prepare filling. Sandwich shells with filling. Store in an airtight container for at least 24 hours before serving.

Cheery Bear Macarons

Makes 40–50 macarons

  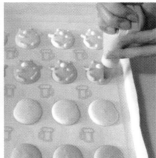 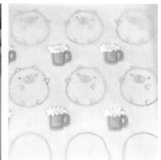

Mass

200 g almond powder

200 g icing sugar

80 g egg whites, at room temperature, divided into 2 portions

Colouring for Mass

1/4 tsp white powder food colouring (optional)

1/2 Tbsp dried blue pea flowers (optional)

Royal blue gel food colouring

Italian Meringue

80 g egg whites, at room temperature

200 g sugar

75 g water

Finishing

Black edible ink marker

Peach lustre dust

Grey, golden yellow and white royal icing (page 29)

Suggested Filling

Matcha white chocolate (page 40) or Earl Grey white chocolate (page 40)

1. Prepare baking tray and bear template (page 124).

2. Prepare mass. Sift together almond powder and icing sugar. Mix well. Divide into 2 equal portions. Sift white powder into one portion, if using. Mix well.

3. Place blue pea flowers into a portion of egg whites and let steep (page 27), if using. Add blue egg whites to plain almond mixture and mix well. Add a little blue gel food colouring to obtain desired shade. Add plain egg whites to white almond mixture. Mix well.

4. Prepare Italian meringue (page 16). Divide into 2 equal portions. Prepare macaron batter (page 18). Fold meringue into each mass.

5. Spoon 3 Tbsp of each batter into piping bags fitted with 3-mm round tips and remainder into piping bags fitted with 6-mm tips.

6. Using batter with larger tips, pipe ovals for bears using template as a guide. Tap tray to release trapped air bubbles. Set aside for 15 minutes or until a thin membrane forms. Using batter with smaller tips, pipe bear's ears, snout and limbs on top shells. Let shells dry (page 20).

7. Bake in a preheated oven at 130°C for 17–22 minutes with tray on bottom rack. Rotate tray halfway through baking. Let shells cool on tray before removing.

8. Use a black edible ink marker to draw bear's features. Use a brush to dab on some peach lustre dust for rosy cheeks, if desired.

9. Prepare some grey, golden yellow and white royal icing. Spoon icing into individual piping bags each fitted with a 1-mm round tip.

10. Trace mug with grey icing. Dry in a 50°C oven with fan mode on for 10 minutes. Pipe beverage with golden yellow icing. Oven-dry for 10 minutes. Pipe a ring of circles for foam with white icing. Oven-dry for 2 hours or until mug is completely dry. Gently peel away baking paper. Attach mugs to bear with a drop of icing. Oven-dry for 10 minutes.

11. Prepare filling. Sandwich shells with filling. Store in an airtight container for at least 24 hours before serving.

Baby Chick Macarons

Makes 35–45 macarons

Mass

200 g almond powder

200 g icing sugar

10 g natural yellow powder (optional)

80 g egg whites, at room temperature

Yellow gel food colouring

Italian Meringue

80 g egg whites, at room temperature

200 g sugar

75 g water

Finishing

Orange royal icing (page 29)

Black edible ink marker

Suggested Filling

Lemon SMBC (page 34) with lemon curd (page 31) centre

---

1. Prepare baking tray and chick template (page 125).

2. Prepare mass. Sift together almond powder, icing sugar and yellow powder, if using. Mix well. Add egg whites and a little yellow gel food colouring to obtain desired shade. Mix well.

3. Prepare Italian meringue (page 16).

4. Prepare macaron batter (page 18). Fold meringue into mass.

5. Spoon batter into a piping bag fitted with a 6-mm round tip.

6. Pipe ovals for chicks onto baking tray using template as a guide. Tap tray to release trapped air bubbles.

7. Let shells dry (page 20).

8. Bake in a preheated oven at 135°C for 17–20 minutes with tray on bottom rack. Rotate tray halfway through baking. Let shells cool on tray before removing.

9. Prepare some orange royal icing. Dip a toothpick in icing and draw chick's beak and feet on top shells. Use a black edible ink marker to draw chick's eyes.

10. Prepare filling. Sandwich shells with filling. Store in an airtight container and refrigerate for at least 24 hours before serving.

Playful Kitten Macarons

Makes 35–45 macarons

Mass

200 g almond powder

200 g icing sugar

$\frac{1}{2}$ tsp white powder food colouring (optional)

80 g egg whites, at room temperature

Italian Meringue

80 g egg whites, at room temperature

200 g sugar

75 g water

Finishing

Brown, grey and black royal icing (page 29)

Black and pink edible ink markers

Suggested Filling

Lemon SMBC (page 34) with lemon curd (page 31) centre

Note: Handle these kitten macarons with care as the tails are fragile and may be easily broken.

1. Prepare baking tray and kitten template (page 125).

2. Prepare mass. Sift together almond powder, icing sugar and white powder, if using. Mix well. Add egg whites and mix well.

3. Prepare Italian meringue (page 16).

4. Prepare macaron batter (page 18). Fold meringue into mass.

5. Spoon about $\frac{1}{2}$ cup batter into a piping bag fitted with a 3-mm round tip and remainder into a piping bag fitted with a 6-mm round tip.

6. Using batter with larger tip, pipe ovals for body of kittens onto baking tray using template as a guide. Tap tray to release trapped air bubbles. Set aside for 15 minutes or until a thin membrane forms.

7. Pipe heads with larger tip. Tap tray to release trapped air bubbles.

8. Using batter with smaller tip, pipe short straight lines for legs and long curved lines for tails. Pipe small dots of batter for ears. Use a toothpick to pull batter into shape. Do this only for top shells. Tap tray to release trapped air bubbles .

9. Let shells dry (page 20).

10. Bake in a preheated oven at 130°C for 17–22 minutes with tray on bottom rack. Rotate tray halfway through baking. Let shells cool on tray before removing.

11. Prepare some brown, grey and black royal icing. Spoon icing into individual piping bags each fitted with a 1-mm round tip.

12. Pipe brown and grey patches on kitten's face. Let icing dry before adding eyes with black icing.

13. Use a black edible ink marker or black icing to draw whiskers and mouth. Use a pink edible ink marker to fill in kitten's mouth.

14. Prepare filling. Sandwich shells with filling. Store in an airtight container and refrigerate for at least 24 hours before serving.

Woolly Lamb Macarons

Makes 35–45 macarons

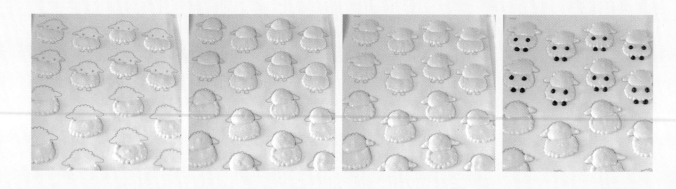

Mass

200 g almond powder

200 g icing sugar

1/2 tsp white powder food colouring (optional)

80 g egg whites, at room temperature

1/2 tsp cocoa powder

1/16 tsp charcoal powder

Italian Meringue

80 g egg whites, at room temperature

200 g sugar

75 g water

Finishing

Pink, light blue and yellow royal icing (page 29)

Black edible ink marker

Suggested Filling

Salted caramel SMBC (page 35) with salted caramel (page 32) centre

---

1. Prepare baking tray and lamb template (page 126).

2. Prepare mass. Sift together almond powder, icing sugar and white powder food colouring, if using. Mix well. Add egg whites and mix well.

3. Prepare Italian meringue (page 16).

4. Prepare macaron batter (page 18). Fold meringue into mass. Spoon 2 Tbsp batter into a small bowl and add cocoa powder. Mix well. Continue folding rest of batter until right consistency is reached.

5. Spoon brown batter into a piping bag fitted with a 2-mm round tip. Spoon 1/2 cup white batter into a piping bag fitted with a 2-mm round tip and remainder into a piping bag fitted with a 5-mm round tip.

6. Using white batter with larger tip, pipe rounded squarish shapes for body of lambs onto baking tray using template as a guide. Using white batter with smaller tip, pipe small circles around lambs for wool, except for neck. Tap tray to release trapped air bubbles. Set aside for 15 minutes or until a thin membrane forms.

7. Using white batter with larger tip, pipe ovals for heads. Using white batter with smaller tip, pipe short lines for ears and small circles around top of heads for wool. Tap tray to release trapped air bubbles.

8. Using brown batter, pipe dots for legs. Use a toothpick to pull batter to desired shape.

9. Let shells dry (page 20).

10. Bake in a preheated oven at 130°C for 17–22 minutes with tray on bottom rack. Rotate tray halfway through baking. Let shells cool on tray before removing.

11. Prepare some pink, light blue and yellow royal icing. Spoon icing into individual piping bags each fitted with a 1-mm round tip. Pipe pink of ears, collar and bell on top shells. Set aside to dry for 1–2 hours.

12. Use a black edible ink marker to draw eyes and nose.

13. Prepare filling. Sandwich shells with filling. Store in an airtight container and refrigerate for at least 24 hours before serving.

Cute Puppy Macarons

Makes 40–50 macarons

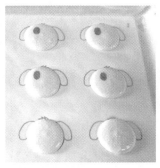

Mass

200 g almond powder

200 g icing sugar

80 g egg whites, at room
temperature

1 tsp + $\frac{1}{4}$ tsp cocoa powder

$\frac{1}{16}$ tsp charcoal powder

Italian Meringue

80 g egg whites, at room
temperature

200 g sugar

75 g water

Finishing

Black royal icing (page 29)

Black edible ink marker

Suggested Filling

Chocolate ganache (page
31) or melted dark chocolate

---

1. Prepare baking tray and puppy template (page 126).

2. Prepare mass. Sift together almond powder and icing sugar.
   Mix well. Add egg whites and mix well.

3. Prepare Italian meringue (page 16).

4. Prepare macaron batter (page 18). Fold meringue into mass.
   Spoon $\frac{1}{4}$ cup batter into a small bowl and add 1 tsp cocoa
   powder and charcoal powder to get a dark brown batter. Mix well.
   Spoon $1\frac{1}{2}$ Tbsp batter into another small bowl and add $\frac{1}{4}$ tsp
   cocoa powder to get a light brown batter. Mix well.

5. Spoon plain batter into a piping bag fitted with a 7-mm round tip,
   dark brown batter into a piping bag fitted with a 4-mm round tip
   and light brown batter into a piping bag fitted with a 3-mm
   round tip.

6. Using plain batter, pipe circles for head of puppies onto baking
   tray using template as a guide, then use light brown batter to
   pipe eye patch on top shells. Tap tray to release trapped air
   bubbles. Use a toothpick to pull batter to create hair on top
   of head. Tap tray again and set aside for 15 minutes until a
   thin membrane forms.

7. Using dark brown batter, pipe ears. Tap tray to release trapped
   air bubbles.

8. Let shells dry (page 20).

9. Bake in a preheated oven at 130°C for 17–22 minutes with tray
   on bottom rack. Rotate tray halfway through baking. Let shells
   cool on tray before removing.

10. Prepare some black royal icing. Spoon icing into a piping bag
    fitted with 1-mm round tip. Pipe noses on top shells. Set aside
    to dry for 1–3 hours.

11. Use a black edible ink marker to draw eyes and mouth on
    top shells.

12. Prepare filling. Sandwich shells with filling. Store in an airtight
    container and refrigerate for at least 24 hours before serving.

Back to Nature

Busy Bee Macarons

Makes 40–50 macarons

Mass

200 g almond powder

200 g icing sugar

80 g egg whites, at room temperature, divided into 60 g and 20 g portions

Colouring for Mass

1½ tsp cocoa powder

12 g charcoal powder

3 g natural yellow powder (optional)

¼ tsp vanilla bean paste (optional)

Black and yellow gel food colouring

Italian Meringue

80 g egg whites, at room temperature

200 g sugar

75 g water

Finishing

White, black and red royal icing (page 29)

Suggested Filling

Cookies & cream SMBC (page 35)

---

1. Prepare baking tray and bee template (page 127).

2. Prepare mass. Sift together almond powder and icing sugar. Mix well. Divide into 300 g and 100 g portions. Sift cocoa and charcoal powders into larger portion and mix well. Sift yellow powder into smaller portion and mix well.

3. Add 60 g egg whites, vanilla bean paste and a little black gel food colouring into larger portion. Mix well. Add 20 g egg whites and yellow gel food colouring into smaller portion. Mix well.

4. Prepare Italian meringue (page 16).

5. Prepare macaron batter (page 18). Fold three-quarters of meringue into black mass. Fold remaining meringue into yellow mass.

6. Spoon black batter into a piping bag fitted with a 6-mm round tip and yellow batter into a piping bag fitted with a 4-mm round tip.

7. Using black batter, pipe circles for bees onto baking tray using template as a guide. Use a toothpick to pull batter to create sting on top shells. Tap tray to release trapped air bubbles. Set aside for 15 minutes or until a thin membrane forms.

8. Using yellow batter, pipe stripes on top shells. Use a toothpick to pull batter into desired shape. Tap tray again.

9. Let shells dry (page 20).

10. Bake in a preheated oven at 135°C for 17–20 minutes with tray on bottom rack. Rotate tray halfway through baking. Let shells cool on tray before removing.

11. Prepare some white, black and red royal icing. Spoon icing into individual piping bags each fitted with a 1-mm round tip.

12. Place bee template under a sheet of baking paper on a baking tray. Use as a guide to pipe bee's wings with white icing. Dry in a 50°C oven with fan mode on for 2 hours or set aside to air-dry. Gently peel away baking paper.

13. Pipe eyes on bee with white icing. Let icing dry completely before adding a dot of black icing. Pipe mouth with red icing.

14. Attach wings onto bees with some icing. Set aside to dry.

15. Prepare filling. Sandwich shells with filling. Store in an airtight container and refrigerate for at least 24 hours before serving.

Pretty Ladybug Macarons

Makes 40–50 macarons

Mass

200 g almond powder

200 g icing sugar

80 g egg whites, at room temperature, divided into 48 g and 32 g portions

Colouring for Mass

1 tsp cocoa powder

10 g charcoal powder

3 g red yeast powder (optional)

$1/8$ tsp vanilla bean paste (optional)

Black and red gel food colouring

2 g beetroot powder (optional)

Italian Meringue

80 g egg whites, at room temperature

200 g sugar

75 g water

Finishing

White, black and red royal icing (page 29)

Black edible ink marker

Suggested Filling

Cookies & cream SMBC (page 35)

---

1. Prepare baking tray and ladybug template (page 127).

2. Prepare mass. Sift together almond powder and icing sugar. Mix well. Divide into 240 g and 160 g portions. Sift cocoa and charcoal powders into larger portion and mix well. Sift red yeast powder into smaller portion and mix well.

3. Mix vanilla bean paste and a little black gel food colouring into 48 g egg whites. Add to larger portion of almond mixture and mix well.

4. Dissolve beetroot powder in 32 g egg whites. Add some red gel food colouring. Add to smaller portion of almond mixture and mix well.

5. Prepare Italian meringue (page 16).

6. Prepare macaron batter (page 18). Fold three-fifths of meringue into black mass. Fold remaining meringue into red mass.

7. Spoon 2 Tbsp black batter into a piping bag fitted with a 3-mm round tip and remaining black batter into a piping bag fitted with a 6-mm round tip. Spoon red batter into a piping bag fitted with a 6-mm round tip.

8. Using black batter, pipe circles for bottom shells onto baking tray using template as a guide.

9. Using red batter, pipe ladybug's wings, then use black batter to pipe heads. Use a toothpick to pull and shape batter so head and wings meet. Tap tray to release trapped air bubbles. Set aside for 15 minutes or until a thin membrane forms.

10. Using black batter with smaller tip, pipe spots on wings. Tap tray to release trapped air bubbles.

11. Let shells dry (page 20).

12. Bake in a preheated oven at 140°C for 16–20 minutes with tray on bottom rack. Rotate tray halfway through baking. Let shells cool on tray before removing.

13. Prepare some white, black and red royal icing. Spoon icing into individual piping bags each fitted with a 1-mm round tip. Pipe eyes with white icing. Let icing dry completely before adding a dot of black icing. Pipe mouth with red icing. Set aside to dry.

14. Use a black edible ink marker to define wings.

15. Prepare filling. Sandwich shells with filling. Store in an airtight container and refrigerate for at least 24 hours before serving.

Fluffy Cloud Macarons

Makes 40–50 macarons

Mass

200 g almond powder

200 g icing sugar

$\frac{1}{2}$ tsp white powder food colouring (optional)

80 g egg whites, at room temperature

White gel food colouring (optional)

Italian Meringue

80 g egg whites, at room temperature

200 g sugar

75 g water

Suggested Filling

Lemon SMBC (page 34) with lemon curd (page 31) centre

---

1. Prepare baking tray and cloud template (page 128).

2. Prepare mass. Sift together almond powder, icing sugar and white powder food colouring, if using. Mix well. Add egg whites and a little white gel food colouring, if using. Mix well.

3. Prepare Italian meringue (page 16).

4. Prepare macaron batter (page 18). Fold meringue into mass.

5. Spoon batter into a piping bag fitted with a 6-mm round tip.

6. Pipe clouds onto baking tray using template as a guide. Start by piping a series of 6 mounds of batter, then fill in centre before lifting off piping tip.

7. Tap tray to release trapped air bubbles. Let shells dry (page 20).

8. Bake in a preheated oven at 130°C for 17–22 minutes with tray on bottom rack. Rotate tray halfway through baking. Let shells cool on tray before removing.

9. Prepare filling. Sandwich shells with filling. Store in an airtight container and refrigerate for at least 24 hours before serving.

Enchanted Rainbow Macarons

Makes 15–20 macarons

Mass

200 g almond powder

200 g icing sugar

80 g egg whites, at room
   temperature

Red, orange, yellow, green
   and blue gel food colouring

Italian Meringue

80 g egg whites, at room
   temperature

200 g sugar

75 g water

Suggested Filling

Lemon SMBC (page 34) with
lemon curd (page 31) centre

---

1. Prepare baking tray and rainbow template (page 128).

2. Prepare mass. Sift together almond powder and icing sugar.
   Mix well. Add egg whites and mix well.

3. Divide mass into 5 equal portions and colour each portion a
   different colour.

4. Prepare Italian meringue (page 16). Divide into 5 equal portions.

5. Prepare macaron batter (page 18). Fold a portion of meringue
   into each mass.

6. Spoon batters into individual piping bags each fitted with a 4-mm
   round tip.

7. Pipe rainbows onto baking tray. Start by piping a series of arcs
   using the various colours as desired. Tap tray to release trapped
   air bubbles.

8. Let shells dry (page 20).

9. Bake in a preheated oven at 135°C for 17–20 minutes with tray
   on bottom rack, then 120°C for 5–10 minutes. Rotate tray halfway
   through baking. Let shells cool on tray before removing.

10. Prepare filling. Sandwich shells with filling. Store in an airtight
   container and refrigerate for at least 24 hours before serving.

Apple Tree Macarons

Makes 35–45 macarons

Mass

200 g almond powder

200 g icing sugar

80 g egg whites, at room temperature, divided into 55 g and 25 g portions

Colouring for Mass

6 g matcha powder

6 g cocoa powder

Green gel food colouring

1/8 tsp vanilla bean paste (optional)

Italian Meringue

80 g egg whites, at room temperature

200 g sugar

75 g water

Finishing

Red royal icing (page 29)

Brown edible ink marker

Suggested Filling

Matcha SMBC (page 35) for foliage and chocolate SMBC (page 34) for tree trunks

---

Note: You may under fold the macaron batter a little to create a macaron shell with a rough surface that mimics the texture of tree trunks and gives the foliage a 3D feel.

1. Prepare baking tray and apple tree template (page 129).

2. Prepare mass. Sift together almond powder and icing sugar. Mix well. Divide into 275 g and 125 g portions.

3. Sift matcha powder into larger portion and mix well. Sift cocoa powder into smaller portion and mix well.

4. Add 55 g egg whites and a little green gel food colouring to matcha almond mixture and mix well. Add 25 g egg whites and vanilla bean paste to cocoa almond mixture and mix well.

5. Prepare Italian meringue (page 16).

6. Prepare macaron batter (page 18). Fold two-thirds of meringue into matcha mass and one-third into cocoa mass.

7. Spoon batters into individual piping bags each fitted with a 5-mm round tip.

8. Using cocoa batter, pipe slim rectangles for tree trunks onto baking tray using template as a guide. Use a toothpick to pull batter to form the shape of tree trunks.

9. Using matcha batter, pipe a series of 7 mounds of batter to form foliage, then fill in centre before lifting off piping tip.

10. Tap tray to release trapped air bubbles. Let shells dry (page 20).

11. Bake in a preheated oven at 140°C for 16–20 minutes with tray on bottom rack. Rotate tray halfway through baking. Let shells cool on tray before removing.

12. Prepare some red royal icing. Spoon into a piping bag fitted with a 1-mm round tip and pipe dots for apples. Dry in a 50°C oven with fan mode on for 1 hour or set aside to air-dry.

13. Use a brown edible ink marker to draw apple stems if desired.

14. Prepare filling. Sandwich shells with filling. Store in an airtight container and refrigerate for at least 24 hours before serving.

Under the Sea

Jumping Dolphin Macarons

Makes 35–45 macarons

Mass

200 g almond powder

200 g icing sugar

80 g egg whites, at room temperature

Colouring for Mass

1 Tbsp dried blue pea flowers (optional)

Teal and white gel food colouring

Italian Meringue

80 g egg whites, at room temperature

200 g sugar

75 g water

Finishing

Black edible ink marker

Suggested Filling

Lavender SMBC (page 36) or chocolate ganache (page 31)

1. Prepare baking tray and dolphin template (page 129).

2. Prepare mass. Sift together almond powder and icing sugar. Mix well.

3. Place blue pea flowers into egg whites for mass and let steep (page 27), if using. Add blue egg whites to almond mixture and mix well. Add a little teal gel food colouring to obtain desired shade. Mix well.

4. Prepare Italian meringue (page 16).

5. Prepare macaron batter (page 18). Fold meringue into mass in 2 additions until no trace of meringue is seen, but batter is still under-folded. Spoon 4 Tbsp batter into a small bowl and add a little white gel food colouring. Continue to fold both batters until right consistency is reached.

6. Spoon light coloured batter into a piping bag fitted with a 3-mm round tip and dark coloured batter into a piping bag fitted with a 5-mm round tip.

7. Using light coloured batter, pipe a slim arc for belly of dolphins on baking tray using template as a guide. Using dark coloured batter, pipe body of dolphin, excluding upper fin. Use a toothpick to pull batter into shape. Pipe blow hole with light coloured batter. Do this for top shells.

8. Using dark coloured batter, pipe whole body of dolphins for bottom shells. Use a toothpick to pull batter into shape.

9. Tap tray to release trapped air bubbles. Set aside for 15 minutes or until a thin membrane forms.

10. Pipe upper fin on top shells. Let shells dry (page 20).

11. Bake in a preheated oven at 135°C for 17–20 minutes with tray on bottom rack. Rotate tray halfway through baking. Let shells cool on tray before removing.

12. Use a black edible ink marker to draw eyes and mouth.

13. Prepare filling. Sandwich shells with filling. Store in an airtight container and refrigerate for at least 24 hours before serving.

Jolly Crab Macarons

Makes 40–50 macarons

Mass

200 g almond powder

200 g icing sugar

8 g red yeast powder (optional)

5 g beetroot powder (optional)

80 g egg whites, at room temperature

Red gel food colouring

Italian Meringue

80 g egg whites, at room temperature

200 g sugar

75 g water

Finishing

White, black and red royal icing (page 29)

Black edible ink marker

> ### Suggested Filling
>
> Salted egg yolk SMBC (page 35)

1. Prepare baking tray and crab template (page 130).

2. Prepare mass. Sift together almond powder, icing sugar and red yeast powder, if using. Mix well. Dissolve beetroot powder in 80 g egg whites. Add red egg whites and red gel colouring to almond mixture and mix well.

3. Prepare Italian meringue (page 16).

4. Prepare macaron batter (page 18). Fold meringue into mass.

5. Spoon about 4 Tbsp batter into a piping bag fitted with a 3-mm round tip and remainder into a piping bag fitted with a 6-mm round tip.

6. Using larger tip, pipe ovals for body of crab on baking tray using template as a guide. Tap tray to release trapped air bubbles.

7. Using smaller tip, pipe pincers and legs for top shells. Use a toothpick to pull batter into shape.

8. Let shells dry (page 20).

9. Bake in a preheated oven at 140°C for 16–20 minutes with tray on bottom rack. Rotate tray halfway through baking. Let shells cool on tray before removing.

10. Prepare some white, black and red royal icing. Spoon icing into individual piping bags each fitted with a 1-mm round tip. Pipe eyes with white icing. Let icing dry completely before adding a dot of black icing.

11. Use black icing or a black edible ink marker to draw mouth. Set aside to dry.

12. Prepare filling. Sandwich shells with filling. Store in an airtight container and refrigerate for at least 24 hours before serving.

Sunny Starfish Macarons

Makes 40–50 macarons

Mass

200 g almond powder

200 g icing sugar

10 g natural yellow powder (optional)

80 g egg whites, at room temperature

Golden yellow gel food colouring

Italian Meringue

80 g egg whites, at room temperature

200 g sugar

75 g water

Finishing

White, black and orange royal icing (page 29)

Black edible ink marker

Suggested Filling

Lemon white chocolate (page 39)

---

1. Prepare baking tray and starfish template (page 130).

2. Prepare mass. Sift together almond powder, icing sugar and yellow powder, if using. Mix well. Add egg whites and a little yellow gel colouring to obtain desired colour. Mix well.

3. Prepare Italian meringue (page 16).

4. Prepare macaron batter (page 18). Fold meringue into mass.

5. Spoon batter into a piping bag fitted with a 5-mm round tip.

6. Pipe 5 triangles to form starfish on baking tray using template as a guide. Fill in centre. Use a toothpick to pull batter into shape. Tap tray to release trapped air bubbles.

7. Let shells dry (page 20).

8. Bake in a preheated oven at 135°C for 17–20 minutes with tray on bottom or second lowest rack. Rotate tray halfway through baking. Let shells cool on tray before removing.

9. Prepare some white, black and orange royal icing. Spoon icing into individual piping bags each fitted with a 1-mm round tip. Pipe eyes with white icing. Let icing dry completely before adding a dot of black icing. Pipe lines on starfish using orange icing. Set aside to dry.

10. Use a black edible ink marker to draw mouth.

11. Prepare filling. Sandwich shells with filling. Store in an airtight container for at least 24 hours before serving.

Pearl in Shell Macarons

Makes 40–50 macarons

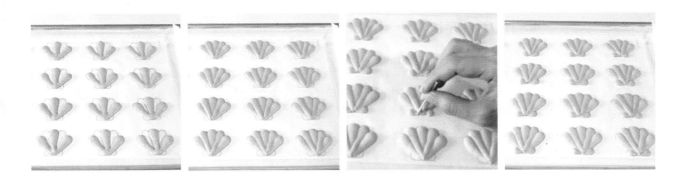

Mass

200 g almond powder

200 g icing sugar

80 g egg whites, at room temperature

Colouring for Mass

1 Tbsp dried blue pea flowers (optional)

Teal gel food colouring

Italian Meringue

80 g egg whites, at room temperature

200 g sugar

75 g water

Finishing

Round white candy or white chocolate balls

Suggested Filling

Rose SMBC (page 36)

1. Prepare baking tray and seashell template (page 131).

2. Prepare mass. Sift together almond powder and icing sugar. Mix well.

3. Place blue pea flowers into egg whites for mass and let steep (page 27), if using. Add blue egg whites to almond mixture and mix well. Add a little teal gel food colouring to obtain desired shade. Mix well.

4. Prepare Italian meringue (page 16).

5. Prepare macaron batter (page 18). Fold meringue into mass.

6. Spoon batter into a piping bag fitted with a 5-mm round tip.

7. Pipe seashell onto baking tray using template as a guide. Start by piping first, third and fifth lines for shell. Tap tray to release trapped air bubbles. Set aside for 10 minutes or until a thin membrane forms.

8. Pipe second and fourth lines. Pipe two small triangles on base of shell, one on the left and another on the right. Tap tray to release trapped air bubbles.

9. Let shells dry (page 20).

10. Bake in a preheated oven at 135°C for 17–20 minutes with tray on bottom rack. Rotate tray halfway through baking. Let shells cool on tray before removing.

11. Prepare filling. Sandwich shells with filling and embed a round candy or chocolate ball in filling for the pearl. Store in an airtight container and refrigerate for at least 24 hours before serving.

Adorable Octopus Macarons

Makes 40–50 macarons

Mass

200 g almond powder

200 g icing sugar

15 g purple sweet potato powder (optional)

80 g egg whites, at room temperature

Purple gel food colouring

Italian Meringue

80 g egg whites, at room temperature

200 g sugar

75 g water

Finishing

Black and blue royal icing (page 29)

Black edible ink marker

> ### Suggested Filling
> Lavender SMBC (page 36)

1. Prepare baking tray and octopus template (page 131).

2. Prepare mass. Sift together almond powder, icing sugar and purple sweet potato powder if using. Mix well. Add egg whites and a little purple gel colouring to obtain desired colour. Mix well.

3. Prepare Italian meringue (page 16).

4. Prepare macaron batter (page 18). Fold meringue into mass.

5. Spoon half the batter into a piping bag fitted with a 4-mm round tip and the other half into a piping bag fitted with a 6-mm round tip.

6. Using larger tip, pipe ovals for head of octopus onto baking tray using template as a guide. Using smaller tip, pipe arms of octopus. Tap tray to release trapped air bubbles.

7. Let shells dry (page 20).

8. Bake in a preheated oven at 135°C for 17–20 minutes with tray on bottom rack. Rotate tray halfway through baking. Let shells cool on tray before removing.

9. Prepare some black and blue royal icing. Spoon into individual piping bags each fitted with a 1-mm round tip. Pipe eyes with black icing and suckers with blue icing. Set aside to dry.

10. Use a black edible ink marker to draw mouth.

11. Prepare filling. Sandwich shells with filling. Store in an airtight container and refrigerate for at least 24 hours before serving.

Design Templates

Use these templates to guide you in piping the macarons. Make a photocopy of your chosen design and enlarge it by 200%. Place the template on the baking tray and place a sheet of baking paper over it before piping. The template can be kept and reused each time you bake.

Colourful Balloons Macaron Pops (page 48)
Enlarge 200%

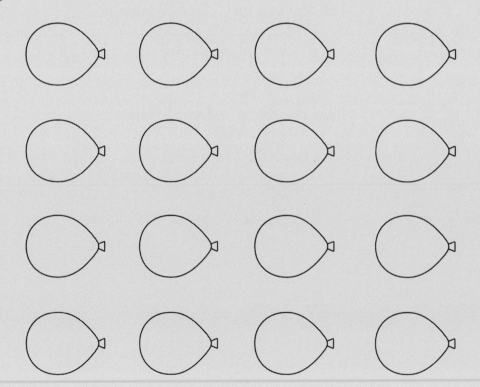

Teacup Macarons (page 50)
Enlarge 200%

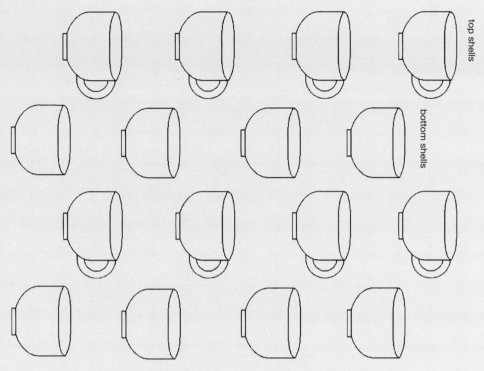

top shells

bottom shells

Colour Pencil Macarons (page 52)
Enlarge 200%

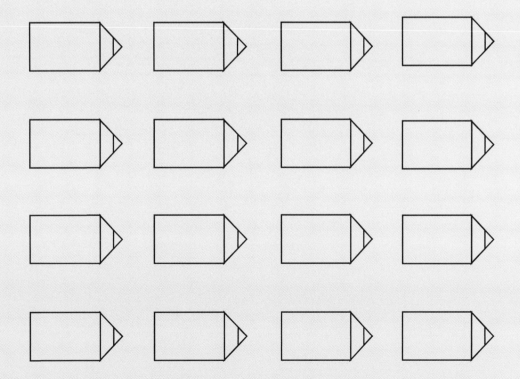

Pretty Clothing Macarons (page 54)
Enlarge 200%

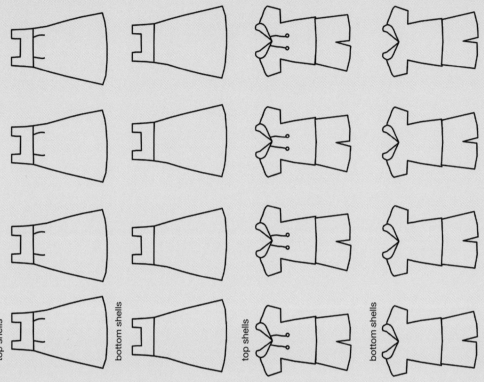

top shells   bottom shells   top shells   bottom shells

Strawberry Ice Cream Cone Macarons (page 56)
Enlarge 200%

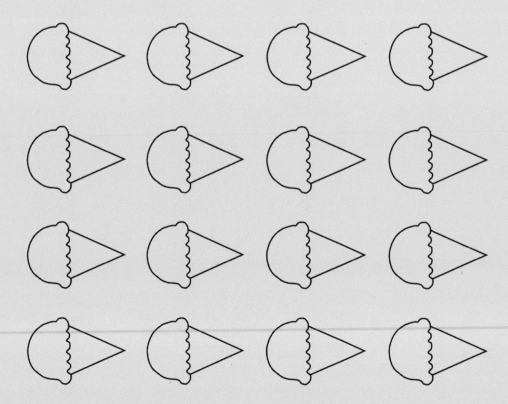

Frosted Cupcake Macarons (page 58)
Enlarge 200%

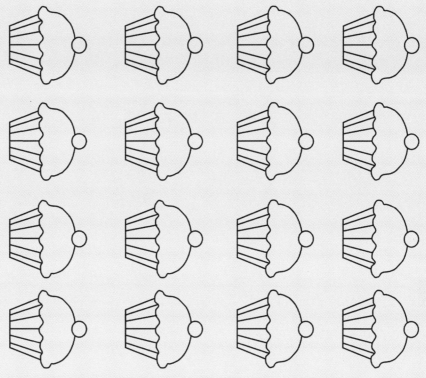

Watermelon Wedges Macarons (page 60)
Enlarge 200%

Traffic Light Macaron Pops (page 66)
Enlarge 200%

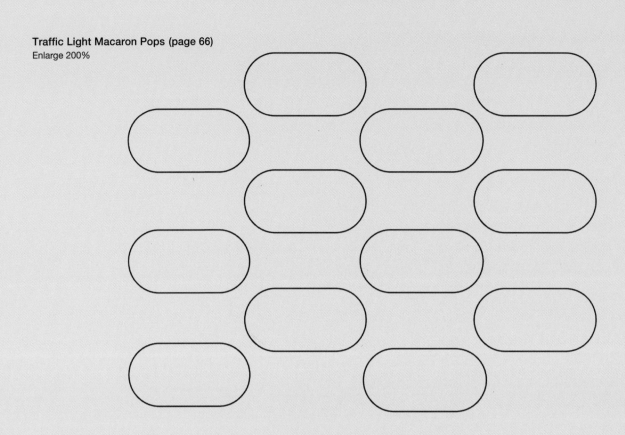

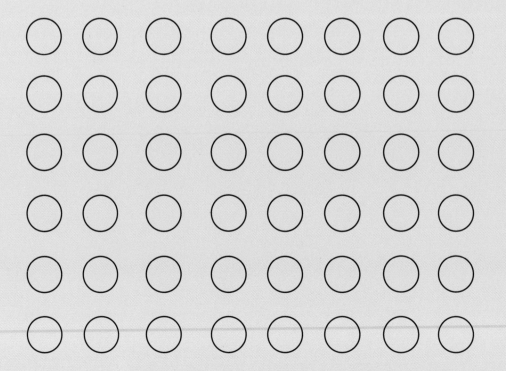

Juicy Carrot Macarons (page 62)
Enlarge 200%

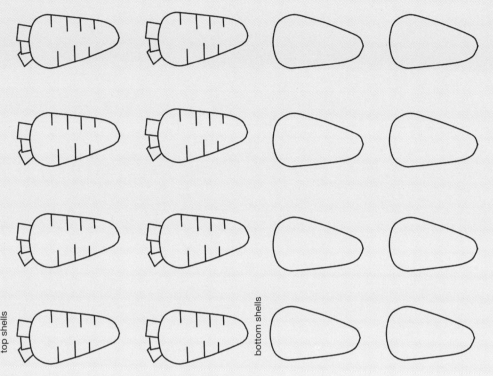

top shells

bottom shells

Speedy Car Macarons (page 68)
Enlarge 200%

top shells

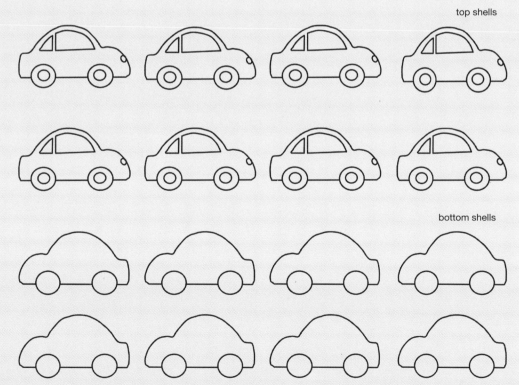

bottom shells

Choo-choo Train Macarons (page 70)
Enlarge 200%

top shells

bottom shells

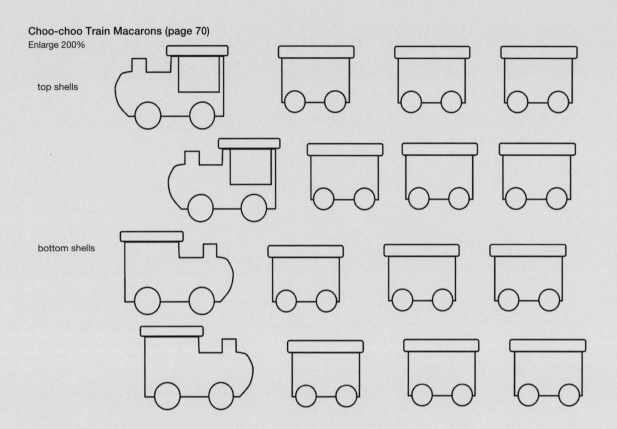

Cruise Ship Macarons (page 72)
Enlarge 200%

top shells

bottom shells

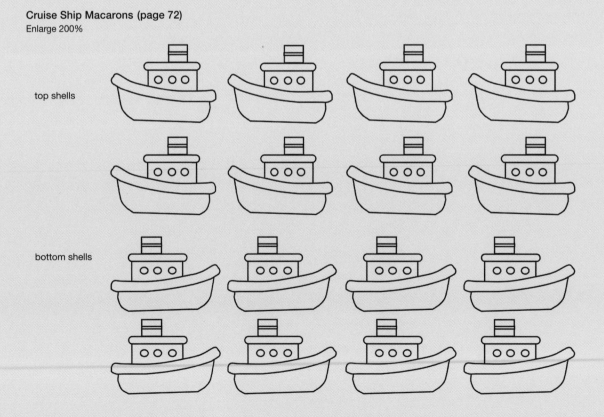

Aircraft Macarons (page 74)
Enlarge 200%

top shells

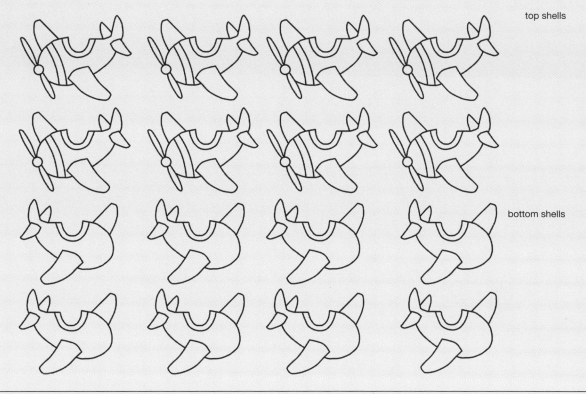

bottom shells

Galloping Horse Macarons (page 78)
Enlarge 200%

top shells

bottom shells

Happy Elephant Macarons (page 80)
Enlarge 200%

top shells

bottom shells

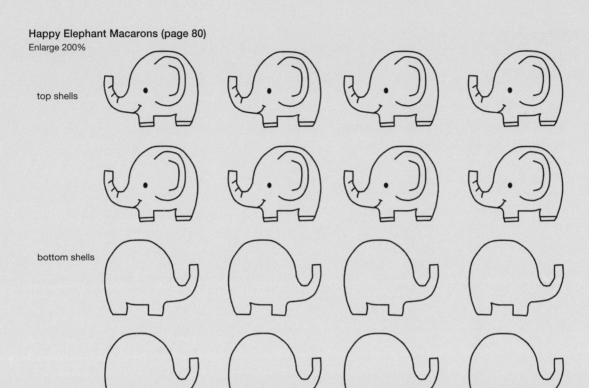

Cheery Bear Macarons (page 82)
Enlarge 200%

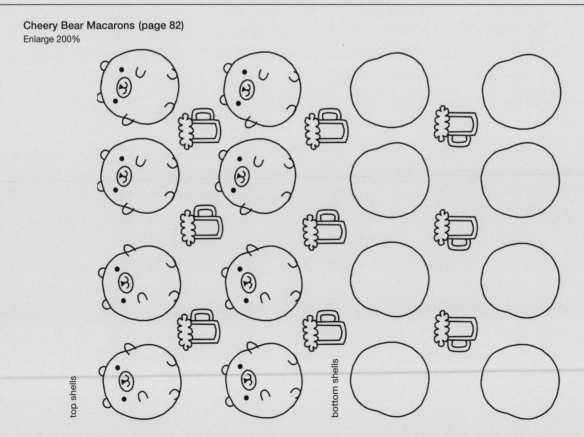

top shells

bottom shells

Baby Chick Macarons (page 84)
Enlarge 200%

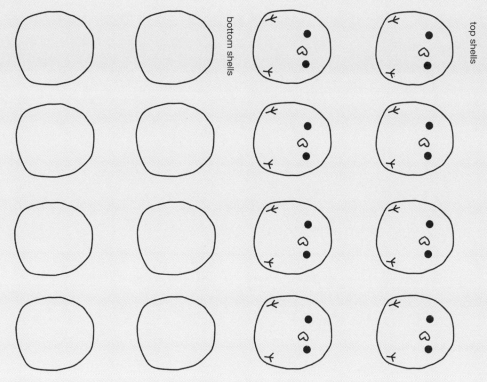

bottom shells

top shells

Playful Kitten Macarons (page 86)
Enlarge 200%

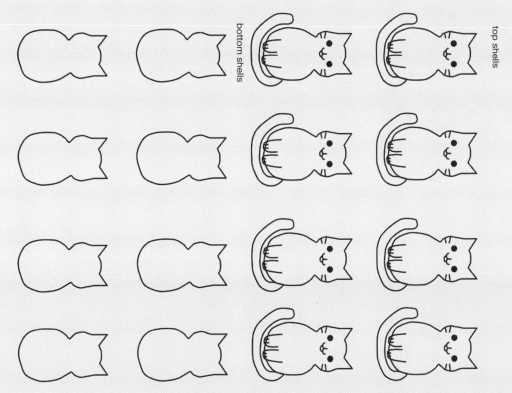

bottom shells

top shells

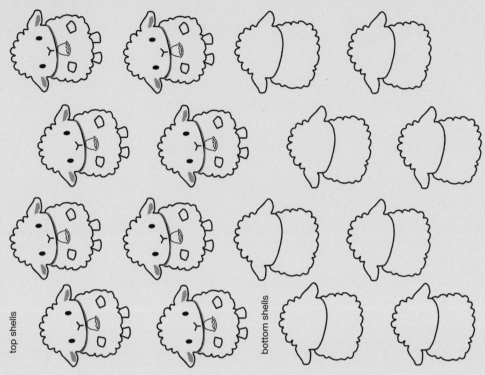

top shells

bottom shells

top shells

bottom shells

Busy Bee Macarons (page 94)
Enlarge 200%

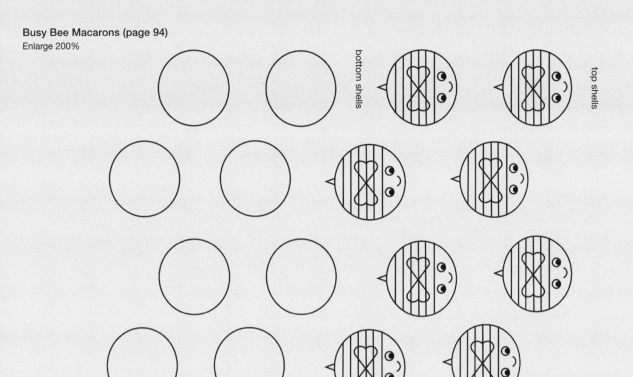

bottom shells

top shells

Pretty Ladybug Macarons (page 96)
Enlarge 200%

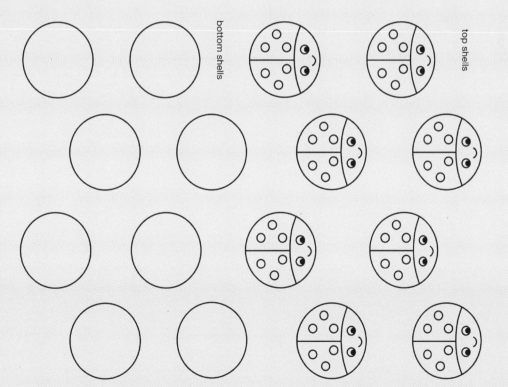

bottom shells

top shells

Fluffy Cloud Macarons (page 98)
Enlarge 200%

Enchanted Rainbow Macarons (page 100)
Enlarge 200%

Apple Tree Macarons (page 102)
Enlarge 200%

bottom shells

top shells

Jumping Dolphin Macarons (page 106)
Enlarge 200%

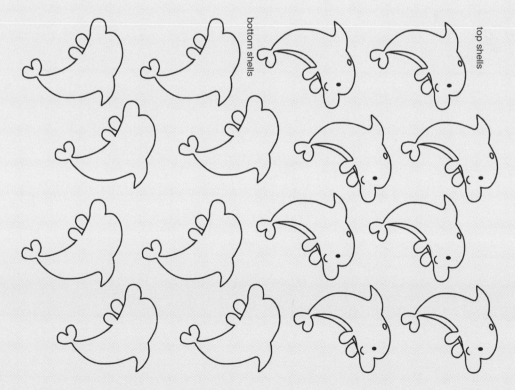

bottom shells

top shells

Jolly Crab Macarons (page 108)
Enlarge 200%

top shells

bottom shells

Sunny Starfish Macarons (page 110)
Enlarge 200%

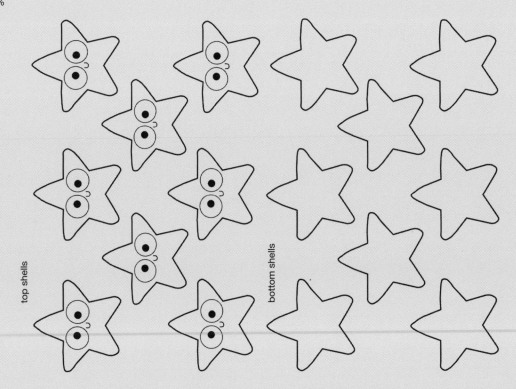

top shells

bottom shells

Pearl in Shell Macarons (page 112)
Enlarge 200%

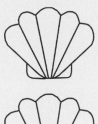

Adorable Octopus Macarons (page 114)
Enlarge 200%

bottom shells

top shells

Weights & Measures

Quantities for this book are given in Metric and American (spoon and cup) measures. Standard spoon and cup measurements used are: 1 teaspoon = 5 ml, 1 tablespoon = 15 ml and 1 cup = 250 ml. All measures are level unless otherwise stated.

LIQUID AND VOLUME MEASURES

Metric	Imperial	American
5 ml	1/6 fl oz	1 teaspoon
10 ml	1/3 fl oz	1 dessertspoon
15 ml	1/2 fl oz	1 tablespoon
60 ml	2 fl oz	1/4 cup (4 tablespoons)
85 ml	2 1/2 fl oz	1/3 cup
90 ml	3 fl oz	3/8 cup (6 tablespoons)
125 ml	4 fl oz	1/2 cup
180 ml	6 fl oz	3/4 cup
250 ml	8 fl oz	1 cup
300 ml	10 fl oz (1/2 pint)	1 1/4 cups
375 ml	12 fl oz	1 1/2 cups
435 ml	14 fl oz	1 3/4 cups
500 ml	16 fl oz	2 cups
625 ml	20 fl oz (1 pint)	2 1/2 cups
750 ml	24 fl oz (1 1/5 pints)	3 cups
1 litre	32 fl oz (1 3/5 pints)	4 cups
1.25 litres	40 fl oz (2 pints)	5 cups
1.5 litres	48 fl oz (2 2/5 pints)	6 cups
2.5 litres	80 fl oz (4 pints)	10 cups

OVEN TEMPERATURE

	°C	°F	Gas Regulo
Very slow	120	250	1
Slow	150	300	2
Moderately slow	160	325	3
Moderate	180	350	4
Moderately hot	190/200	370/400	5/6
Hot	210/220	410/440	6/7
Very hot	230	450	8
Super hot	250/290	475/550	9/10

DRY MEASURES

Metric	Imperial
30 grams	1 ounce
45 grams	1 1/2 ounces
55 grams	2 ounces
70 grams	2 1/2 ounces
85 grams	3 ounces
100 grams	3 1/2 ounces
110 grams	4 ounces
125 grams	4 1/2 ounces
140 grams	5 ounces
280 grams	10 ounces
450 grams	16 ounces (1 pound)
500 grams	1 pound, 1 1/2 ounces
700 grams	1 1/2 pounds
800 grams	1 3/4 pounds
1 kilogram	2 pounds, 3 ounces
1.5 kilograms	3 pounds, 4 1/2 ounces
2 kilograms	4 pounds, 6 ounces

LENGTH

Metric	Imperial
0.5 cm	1/4 inch
1 cm	1/2 inch
1.5 cm	3/4 inch
2.5 cm	1 inch

ABBREVIATION

tsp	teaspoon
Tbsp	tablespoon
g	gram
kg	kilogram
ml	millilitre